**Theory and Methods
in
Dance-Movement Therapy**

Theory and Methods
in
Dance-Movement Therapy

A MANUAL FOR THERAPISTS,
STUDENTS, AND EDUCATORS

SECOND EDITION

Penny Lewis Bernstein

Registered Dance Therapist
Antioch Graduate School
Keene, New Hampshire

KENDALL/HUNT PUBLISHING COMPANY
DUBUQUE, IOWA

Copyright © 1972, 1975 by Penny Lewis Bernstein

ISBN 0—8403—0615—6

Printed in the United States of America

To Lynne, Ann, Judy, and Irma

CONTENTS

Chapter

Appendix

Dance-Movement Therapy is a relatively young profession in the field of mental health. And, like all viable entities, it has struggled and is continuing to struggle through a maturational process. All infancy can be seen as involving both a striving toward the integration of various perceptions of the environment coupled with the experimenting with responses either through accomodation or adaptation. In the case of Dance-Movement Therapy the "environment" can be defined as the individual or group to be evaluated and treated while the "responses" take the form of ways of relating to and modifying the client's(') behavior.

Dance Therapy is now in its adolescence. Characteristically, this period of development entails the ability to think reflectively and to combine and synthesize experience. It is also a time to evolve an identity—a sense of self. In other words it is time now to gather all previous perceptions, techniques, concepts, etc. in Dance Therapy and to synthesize them into one congruent functioning whole under one frame of reference. By providing a theoretical base upon which both existing and new observational data and techniques can be placed, Dance-Movement Therapy can become an integrated totality.

It is toward this undertaking that this manual attends itself. This book is the author's first attempt at ordering thoughts and coming to grips with the relationship between movement analysis and psychological concepts. It does not by any means preport to be the final word in Dance-Movement Therapy; it is rather "a" word, a way of looking at this field which has grown from education and experience. It is an in depth analysis which synthesizes the basic components of Dance-Movement Therapy into a coherent and comprehensive system.

It cannot be emphasized enough that this book is not in any way a "cook book." "Cook books" in the field of human behavior do gross injustice to the subject matter as well as to those involved. Examples are given of certain ways of looking at maladaptive behavior and treatment. They are as stated: examples—one possibility among many. It is hoped also that all elements discussed will be seen within the context of the sequence of the characteristic movement repertoire of the client and as they relate to the total human being and his way of life.

The theoretical frame of reference which has been selected was chosen due to its applicability and relevance with existing data in this field as well as its success in other areas of mental health and neurophysiologic rehabilitation. The theory utilized is that of the recapitulation of ontogeny, i.e., the repetition of the basic elements in life which are thought to be responsible for normal development. It is built on the premise that any individual who has difficulty functioning adequately in body movement will be able to live more successfully by organizing and integrating those components in psycho-motor maturation which are usually learned in the normal growth process.

Dance-Movement Therapy is seen as a means of assisting individual(s) through movement to develop and organize a repertoire of behavior which will enable the person or persons to satisfy their own needs and adjust adequately to the demands of the environment.

It is important also to note here that because of its developmental base, this book is applicable not only to the dance therapist but to the person who is involved with the primary prevention of psycho-motor pathology: the physical educator.

Penny Lewis Bernstein MA, OTR, DTR

ACKNOWLEDGMENTS

I could not have even begun to conceptualize the possibility of writing this book if it were not for the excellence of my teachers. Dr. Ann Mosey is not a dance or movement therapist; however, if one were to glance over the footnotes, one would find that much came from Ann's ideas in her work in Occupational Therapy. What I have tried to do is to give to Dance-Movement Therapy some of the clarity of information concerning this field with the utilization of the recapitulation theory that Ann had given in her field of O.T.

Without the many hours spent by Dr. Judith Kestenberg going over and reinforcing her way of evaluating and looking at development through movement much of this book would have suffered. Thank you Judy.

To my other teachers: Lynne Berger, Marian Chace, Claire Schmais, Al Lowen, and the forever understanding Irmgard Bartenieff who has taken time out of her busy schedule to go over and over the manuscript with me, go my whole-hearted appreciation.

Richard Noel's creative photography has greatly clarified and enhanced this manual. And, as I do not believe in photographing my patients, I thank my friends and fellow mental health workers for taking part in movement sessions. I particularly want to thank my fellow dance therapists: Donna Hallen, Rita Drapkin, and Mary Jo Simasek who worked many hours with me on the individual illustrations.

And last, but by no means least: To my clients who taught me what no book or course could ever begin to, thank you all.

P.L.B.

CHAPTER I

Dance-Movement Therapy:
Its Rationale and the Development
of a Theoretical Frame of Reference

Every human, however reserved or quiet whether at rest or in overt movement, is always engaged in motion. This rhythmic motility or "dancing" as it has sometimes been called is a direct means of expression. It is often more direct than verbalization, for its origin quite often stems from an unconscious spontaneous reaction to how the person perceives his environment.

Meerloo in his book on Creativity and Eternalization discusses the everyday "dance" of conversation. A definite rhythmic pattern is manifested in the form of unobtrusive gestures and increases and decreases of breathing, sound vibrations, pauses, and reactions to the verbalizations of others.

Dr. W.C. Condon, who has done extensive research in linguistics and kinesthetics, has found that: "Intensive analysis of sound films has revealed that human behavior is ordered and rhythmical at many levels with respect to both speech and body motion and to personal and interactional behavior. It is this startlingly rhythmical and participant nature of human communication which suggests that human interaction may be inherently dance-like in form."[1]

Interrelationship of Emotional Expression
and Movement[2]

Since Darwin's The Expression of Emotion in Man and Animals, extensive study has been executed concerning the correlation between emotional expression and observed movement. As early as 1932, studies of expressive qualities of body posture were being carried out by William James. He feels that every emotion has its expression in the postural model of the body, and that the changes in this model are connected with expressive attitudes.

[1] W.S. Condon, "Linguistic-Kinesic Research and Dance Therapy," American Dance Therapy Association Conference Proceedings (October, 1968), p. 22.

[2] The definition of the concept of expressive movement as used in this book: Expressive movement refers to those aspects of movement which are distinctive enough to differentiate one individual from another.

In 1943 research carried out by Wolff proved that "bodily forms indicate expressive values for people regardless of their state of mind whether in a normal, mentally diseased, or hypnotic state."[3]

Dunbar draws on an even deeper connection between emotional expression and motion. She feels that unconscious psychic energy is directly utilized to produce movement. "Evidence has been given which suggests that an essential part of mental and emotional activities consists of emotion as we formerly believed; in physical terms, they are the energy of corresponding mental and emotional activity."[4]

Drs. Vernon and Allport feel that there are significant congruences between emotive expression and motor performances which cannot be accounted for by chance or habit, but which occur logically and naturally.[5] They proceed to say that:

"Several theories assume that there are processes of identification, generalization, and spread which result in complex psychodynamic dispositions that exert a dynamic determination upon specific movements. Fundamentally our results lend support to the personalistic contentions that there is some degree of unity (or disunity) in personality, that this unity (or disunity) is reflected in expression, and that, for this reason, acts and habits of expression show a certain consistency among themselves."

What Allport discovered were movement pattern clusters or behavioral sequences which parallel other aspects of the individual's personality. These findings seem to correlate with those of Lamb, Kestenberg, Rothstein and Bartenieff.[6]

It would take a book in itself to discuss all the research that has been carried out in the observation of movement and its emotional content. Renee Spitz's work in the psychoanalytic study of the development of symbolic movement is one example.[7] Felix Deutsch, who names his method of movement observation "analytic posturology" is another.[8]

Bartenieff and Davis on Deutsch, state:[9]

[3] Werner Wolff, The Expression of Personality (New York: Harper Bros., 1945), p. 27.

[4] Flanders Dunbar, Emotions and Bodily Changes (New York: Columbia University Press, 1954), p. 212.

[5] G.W. Allport and P.E. Vernon, Studies of Expressive Movement (New York: Hafner Publishing Company, 1967), p. 121.

[6] Will be mentioned later.

[7] Renee Spitz, No and Yes (New York: International Universities Press, 1957).

[8] Felix Deutsch, "Analytic Posturology and Synthesiology," The Psychoanalytic Review, Vol. 50, No. 1, 1963.

[9] Irmagard Bartenieff and Martha Davis, Effort-Shape Analysis of Movement: The Unity of Expression and Function (New York: Dance Notation Bureau, 1965).

"Deutsch regards postures as unconscious responses to instinctual impulses or sensory perceptions. In explaining the origin of the postures Deutsch states that if the child loses a love-object he may replace it with a symbolic substitute. Thus, certain body parts become invested with symbolic meaning according to their structure or function."

Movement and Its Relationship to Psychotherapy

It is the "observable" relationship between motion and emotion which opens the door to many to the uses of movement as a tool in psychotherapy. However, even before all the above studies and research were carried out, the connection between movement and therapy had been seen and attempts to utilize it were made. Centuries ago, "the play with rhythmic chant and rhythmic movement became a religious rite supposed to liberate man from fear and burdens of separateness and death. The dance of the medicine man, priest, or shaman belongs to the oldest form of medicine and psychotherapy in which the common exaltation and release of tensions was able to change man's physical and mental suffering into a new option on health. We may say that at the dawn of civilization dance and medicine were inseparable."[10]

Today, Dr. Arnheim, author of extensive literature on the relationship between art and psychology, feels that "the fact that expressive behavior is so much more readily accessible to scientific description than are the corresponding physical processes deserves attention. He suggests that in the future, psychologists who undertake the task of reducing complex mental processes to configurations of basic forces may choose the study of behavior as the most suitable method."[11] (And movement is one of the most precise manifestations of behavior to observe.)

Movement as therapy is not only useful in the observation and interpretation of emotion and mental illness but also in the treatment process as well.

Wilhelm Reich was one of the first physicians to become aware of and utilize body posturing and movement in psychotherapy. The well known term "character armor" describing in part the physical manifestation of the way in which an individual deals with anxiety, fear, anger, etc. was utilized by him. Today, however, many psychotherapists: psychiatrists, psychologists, as well as dancers have become aware of and made use of movement's therapeutic qualities.

[10] Joost A. Meerloo, Creativity and Eternization (New York: Humanities Press, 1968), p. 69.

[11] Rudolph Arnheim, Toward a Psychology of Art (Los Angeles: University of California Press, 1966), p. 72.

3

In my opinion, though, the most important rationale for the necessity of movement in psychotherapy is the need to communicate to the patient on his level. There is an extremely large population of individuals who have regressed past (schizophrenic) or have never gotten to (autistic) the verbal level in human development. I can remember very clearly watching a psychiatrist trying unsucessfully to relate on a verbal level to an autistic child. The little girl's reaction was as if he were speaking a foreign language; and, in fact, he was. He was communicating verbally when she was still at a pre-verbal level. The same reaction has occurred with severely regressed patients as well. The fact that these individuals may or may not actually understand what is being said to them is not the point; the point is, however, that like most everyone else, they will interact best on the level at which they feel most comfortable.

The non-verbal level of communication, the level of movements is the major communicative and therapeutic tool that the dance-movement therapist utilizes. This is his milieu; this is where he is the most needed and can do the most good. It is up to the therapist to evolve the patient from the level of solely non-verbal communication to one of verbal communication as well.

The Need for a Frame of Reference

Now more than ever due to the extensive involvement in the field of Movement Therapy the development of a rationale for treatment is of paramount importance. It is not sufficient just to have one or two theories from which to choose. The more points of view presented, the broader the outlook and, hopefully, the greater the validity. Adoption of various elements of each could then occur, resulting, perhaps, in an even better, stronger, eclectic approach.

Dr. Chaiklin has written an article concerning the desperate need for a theory in Dance Therapy. He states that, "the scientist and the artist must have a point of view (a theoretical frame of reference); they must master the tools of their medium; they must be aware that knowledge is tentative and probable; and they must display their work and subject it to the judgement of peers and public."[12]

There are too few theories being offered to those interested in Dance-Movement Therapy. More often than not, techniques and methods are constructed with little or no theoretical frame of reference for a foundation. With the exception of a few philosophies such as Effort-Shape, the presence of a rationale is totally absent. The only vestige of theory that can be seen is a rather loose over-

---

[12] Harris Chaiklin, "Research and the Development of a Profession," American Dance Therapy Association Conference Proceedings (October, 1968), p. 67.

inclusive definition of the major goal of Dance Therapy. Defining concepts is only one aspect of theory building; though essential it is far from being inclusive. Consequently, those who are interested in the field are left with an extremely vague feeling of the functional totality of dance and movement in therapy.

This lack of total understanding extends not only to the dance therapists and their students but to all those surrounding the therapist as well. Communication with doctors, nurses, and others involved in the therapeutic process suffers. The professional quality of Dance-Movement Therapy is severely impaired, and those who could conceivably aid the dance therapist in upgrading the status of the profession and inquire about it are told not about the theory but rather about a few usually unrelated techniques used by the therapist. This leaves the inquirer with a rather general view of some seemingly unrelated methods with no rationale, no frame of reference for a foundation.

Those who suffer worse however, are not the medical and paramedical team or the students or the dance therapists—but the patients themselves. At best the world of a mental patient is one of incongruities and conflicts. With some, ego boundaries are in a state of dissolution bringing with it a sense of fragmentation of mind and body. What they do not need is a grouping of unrelated techniques that may help them that day but that will give them no over-all sense of sequential progression.

The Construction of a Theory:
The Idea and Rationale for Its Use in Dance-Movement Therapy

Of primary importance is to reemphasize the fact that no theoretical frame of reference should be considered the "only one." Other theories should be considered as well if one is to feel fully competent in this field of Dance-Movement Therapy. Nor should anyone feel that the theories extant are all that are needed in this profession. If Movement Therapy is to develop, new ideas must continue to grow and evolve from observation and interpretation of the over-all as well as immediate occurrences.

The formulation of an idea through the synthesis of past experiences and new perceptions is the beginning of the theory building process. Even at this initial level some sort of rationale or raison d'etre should become apparent. There should be sufficient material extant to prove this to be a worthwhile course to follow.

The theory that is being proposed is not a new one to psychotherapy; its beginnings are apparent in the teachings of Freud. It has roots in neurophysiology and in physical rehabilitation such as with the work of Drs. Bobath, Reed, Fay, and Kabot. It was taught to me by one of its catalysts, Dr. Ann Mosey, who utilized it in the field of Occupational Therapy.

5

This theory for the treatment of the psychically and neuro-muscularly ill is based on the idea of the recaptiulation of ontogeny, i.e., the repetition of basic elements in life which are thought to be responsible for normal development. Therapy, then involves the assisting of an individual to integrate and/or organize those vital elements of development which he needs for adaptive functioning.

Because of its use both in psychopathology and in neurology and orthopedics, it is doubly applicable for Dance-Movement Therapy. The dance-movement therapist continually works toward the psycho-motor or body-mind integration of his or her clients. The theory that is used should therefore bear relationship to and be useful therapeutically in both these areas.

Several psychiatrists have proven that this form of therapy is valid. Dr. Marguerite Sechehaye in her Autobiography of a Schizophrenic Girl relates step by step one of the few recorded cures of schizophrenia. The theory she utilized was based on the recapitulation of all factors needed for normal development. Dr. Mosey, resynthesizing the methods utilized by Paul Schilder, an analyst and conceptualizer of the well known term body-image (a vital concern of Dance Therapy), states that, "defective experiences during the developmental process may lead to pathological distortions of body-image. Treatment is then based on the theory that distortion of the body-image may be corrected by providing similar experiences to those believed responsible for the development of an adequate body-image."[13]

Psychoanalysts are, in general, attempting to recapitulate the development of an individual's dyadic relationships through the use of transference. Neurophysiologists and physical therapists utilize this theory primarily with brain damaged individuals such as those diagnosed as cerebral palseyed and the perceptually-motor impaired. Some of the techniques used within this form of treatment involve centering on primitive reflexes and their inhibition; mass, spiral, diagonal patterning, postural reflexes, and the teaching of automatic movements.

The techniques and tools of these therapies are in part different than those of the dance-movement therapist. Is the theory of recapitulation of ontogeny applicable to Dance-Movement Therapy? Besides the author, many therapists as well as those aware of the field, have been drawn to a similar conclusion.

Dr. Dyrud, who assisted Marian Chace in the development of Dance Therapy, states: "Much of the current literature on child development suggests that his route from sensory-motor to cognitive is the normal pattern of growth and development. It is now recog-

---

[13] Ann Mosey, "Treatment of Pathological Distortion of Body Image," American Journal of Occupational Therapy, XXIII (September-October, 1969), p. 413.

nized that the psychomotor development of the child provides the action which is subsequently internalized as thought and feeling." He later suggests recapitulating "the developmental scheme by leading a person deeply alienated from himself and others into a dialogue by steps which begin as simply as daring to stretch and daring to move in relation to the therapist." [14]

Elements of the theory of recapitulation of ontogeny can be found in the theories of dance therapists. Irmgard Bartenieff, a cofounder of the use of Effort-Shape in Dance Therapy, wrote a paper on the exploration of Effort-Shape analysis and philosophy, in conjunction with Martha Davis: "Ultimately the validity of effort-shape assessment of adult movement, normal or pathological rests on the precise study of the development of effort-shape variables through childhood." [15]

Claire Schmais and Elissa White both utilize the Effort-Shape philosophy in the training of dance therapists and in the treatment of patients. They feel that some of the basic goals in this therapy are the development of the same pattern of movement throughout the total body and a broadening of a repertoire of efforts and shapes. Through Dr. Kestenberg's analysis of the roles of movement patterns in development, these goals can be seen as levels in the progression of normal development as well.

Identification and Definition of Concepts and Hypotheses Which Directly Apply to the Theory of Recapitulation of Ontogeny in Dance-Movement Therapy[16]

Concepts

Movement Therapy—A means of assisting individuals through movement to organize and develop a repertoire of behavior which will enable them to satisfy their own needs and adjust adequately to the demands of the environment.

Adaptive Patterns—Those learned components of behavior which an individual employs in order to use his environment (internal as well as external) creatively in adjusting to and satisfying self needs and the demands of the environment.

Developmental Task—The process of learning or organizing an age appropriate adaptive pattern.

---

[14] Jarl Dyrud, Marian Chuce and Jean Erdman, "The Meaning of Movement as Human Expression and as an Artistic Communication," ADTA Conference Proceedings (October 1967), p. 40.

[15] Bartenieff, op. cit., p. 27.

[16] Concepts, hypotheses and theory are extracted and adapted from: Anne Mosey, Occupational Therapy: Theory and Practice (Medford: Pothier Bros. Printers, 1968).

Maladaptive Behavior—Behavior which either does not adequately satisfy the individual's needs and/or demonstrates lack of adjustment to the demands of the environment.

State of Function—An individual may be said to be in a state of function when he has organized in an integrated manner those adaptive patterns which are required in order to satisfy self needs and meet the demands of the environment.

State of Dysfunction—An individual may be said to be in a state of dysfunction when he has not fully organized in an integrated manner those adaptive patterns which are required in order to satisfy self needs and meet the demands of the environment.

Hypotheses

Process of identifying function and dysfunction—The individual's state of function or dysfunction may be assessed through the observation of his motor behavior. Either component-related maladaptive behavior or behavior which exhibits adaptive components may be observed while the individual is participating in total movement activities requiring the use of adaptive patterns.

Movement from a state of dysfunction to function—This development is brought about by participation in total movement activity so structured that it fulfills the prerequisites for learning by providing activity elements which are representational of those environmental elements required for the learning of needed adaptive components.

Summary

The theory of recapitulation of ontogeny states that any individual who has difficulty in functioning adequately in body movement will be able to live more successfully by organizing those adaptive patterns which are usually integrated in normal development. The organizing process may occur in total movement activities which incorporate the components usually acquired in normal human development needed for the purpose of evolving a functioning individual. The specific patterns utilized will depend upon the most basic level at which the individual is able to function; and through various movement activities using higher complexities of development, the therapist, utilizing attributes of previously organized patterns, will evolve the individual to the appropriate level at which he should be functioning. Within this framework, the therapist keeps in mind what is idiosyncratically and socio-culturally adaptive for each individual such that the desired movement repertoire is a natural expression of the individual within his environment.

8

Further Consideration and Application

This theory is easily adaptable to almost any approach utilized in psychotherapy whether it be an intensive care psychoanalytic sanatorium, out-patient community, mental health center, or in private practice. Although the foundations are in neurophysiology and psychotherapy, the theory stresses the practical organizing of socio-economic abilities which are needed in everyday life. Further flexibility is built in the realization that not all individuals need to organize all the adaptive patterns which will be recorded in the following chapter. Treatment plans will be influenced by, among other things, the client's chronological and mental age, his previous cultural socialization, and the socio-economic environment to which he returns.

It should also be noted that although these patterns are sequential, the patient himself determines by his actions and abilities the degree of emphasis placed at each level. Equal time is not always given to each adaptive pattern. This is particularly true when treatment is directed toward a regressed individual who has already partially organized many of the areas. Once early levels, i.e., the foundation is in place, the recapitulation process may progress toward the appropriate level of development at a quicker pace. The end goal and progress for each individual is therefore specifically structured for his own needs and rhythmic patterns of growth.

This theory is not based on the usual nomenclature of medical diagnosis; however, for reasons of familiarity and clarity, the standard classifications will be employed. By definition it would seem that those who are in a state of dysfunction had never integrated or organized the patterns or had attempted to learn them but, due to inadequate integration of a foundation level, were somewhat impeded and ineffectual in functioning at higher and more complex levels. Autistic children, as well as individuals suffering from schizophrenia, seem especially to fall into one of these categories; however, various forms of neurosis such as the anxiety neurosis which is frequently associated with somatic symptoms, the obsessive-compulsive, depressive, neuroasthenic, and depersonalization neurosis involving often a feeling of estrangement from the body can be helped in Movement Therapy. Psychophysiologic disorders with the accompanying somatic symptomatology; behavior disorders of childhood and adolescence such as the hyperkinetic or withdrawal syndrome; as well as certain personality disorders such as the passive-aggressive, schizoid, and asthenic with his low energy level are all conditions which may be treated with the use of Movement Therapy.

Although this theory is specifically designed for the treatment of those in a state of emotional dysfunction by dance-movement therapists, other areas involved with rehabilitation and/or growth might benefit from its utilization. For example, use of this theory may be made in attempting to "re-adapt" culturally deprived children to the types of abilities needed for adequate functioning in a society which stresses other adaptive patterns.

Students in a normal school setting could also benefit from a teacher who is knowledgeable in the underlying age-specific body-movement patterns needed by an individual in order to function adequately. By being able to detect at what level the difficulty in the organization of a behavior or skill becomes apparent, primary and elementary classroom teachers as well as those involved in physical education could be better able to instruct and evolve their students to higher levels of ability and adaptability, utilizing activities which stress psycho-motor organization and integration.

CHAPTER II

The Learning Process

The learning of adaptive patterns is supported by two related concepts in the theory of development: (1) Werner's principles of orthogenesis and (2) Piaget's process of equilibration.

Orthogenesis may be defined as follows:

1. increasing differentiation and specification of primitive action systems causing

2. the emergence of novel discrete action systems that are also increasingly integrated within themselves.

3. The most advanced systems functionally subordinate and regulate less developed systems. [1]

This definition generally states that in the course of normal development action systems become more and more highly complex and differentiated.

Equilibration, on the other hand, is "a process of 'formative instability combined with progressive movement toward stability.' Its course is spiral and consists of 'progressive involutions by which structure and function are jointly matured.'"[2]

When these two concepts are combined, learning can be seen as an active process whereby more and more complex action systems are differentiated and specified causing progressive states of disequilibrium which result, through the need to re-obtain equilibrium, in more complex novel discrete action systems.

Thus, a spiral process of development may be visualized, with each new level of complexity growing out of the last.

Like most developmental theorists, Piaget feels that normal growth is not solely a physiological experience; it is rather an interactional process between the environment and the individual.

[1] Jonas Langer, Theories of Development (New York: Holt, Rinehart and Winston, 1969), p. 92.

[2] Ibid., p. 93.

11

If the environment does not supply the appropriate elements for the learning and integrating of more organized levels, the transition to the next level will be inadequate.

Therefore, in order for the learning of a particular level in functioning to take place, the individual must not only have arrived at a sufficient maturational level, have fully organized all the past—and less complex—levels of functioning, and have progressed into a state of disequilibrium; but he must also be in an adequate and appropriate environment which has all the necessary elements in order for learning to occur.

Barring physical disorders, it should then follow that if the appropriate environment is provided, normal development will occur. Therefore, once the degree of maturation and the most basic level of functioning of the individual have been ascertained by the therapist, the latter may begin to construct the environment which is suitable for the learning process.

The environment formulated by the movement therapist can be seen as either representational and/or symbolic of the appropriate environment needed to fully integrate a higher level of functioning. It is comprised of a total movement activity which involves the preparation, preoccupation, recognition and retreat of all those pertinent adaptive patterns.

CHAPTER III

Developmental Constellation

The following 16 areas of organization will give the reader an idea of the various ways of looking at ontogeny and the corresponding levels of development which can be organized through participation in total movement activities. It is hoped that although these areas are discussed separately, they will nevertheless be seen as interrelated horizontally (among the 16 areas) as well as vertically (within each developmental line). It has been shown that dysfunction in one area affects other areas of psycho-social development. For example, if an individual is unable to organize the ability to be aware of body parts and their relationship (body-image area), he will very probably have a great deal of difficulty shaping his body in relation to the environment (shape area).

It should also be noted that more than one adaptive level may be integrated or organized during a total movement activity. In fact, it is almost impossible to separate related components of the developmental levels of organization if the individual is to be involved in an adequate environment for learning. For example, the therapist could not expect to evolve the patient from investment of positive affect in self and others to investment of aggressive drive in external objects (drive-object area) without the appropriate dyadic relationship. Anna Freud states, "If we examine our notions of average normality in detail, we find that we expect a fairly close correspondence between growth on the developmental lines. In clinical terms this means that, to be a harmonious person, a child who has reached a specific stage in the sequence toward emotional maturity, should have attained also corresponding levels in his growth toward bodily independence, in the lines toward companionship, constructive play, etc."[1]

It is also important to clarify the fact that all levels of organization within each of the developmental lines continue throughout life. For example, a person is still aware of the relationship of

[1] Anna Freud, M.D., Normality and Pathology in Childhood (New York: International Universities Press, 1966), pp. 84-85.

his body parts after he has organized the ability to move through space adaptively. [2]

Each developmental line of levels of organization will be divided as follows:

1. A brief summary of the relevance of the developmental levels of organization in Dance-Movement Therapy.

2. A hierarchical outline of the levels of organization.

3. Related maladaptive behavior with suggested methods and techniques for Dance-Movement Therapy.

4. Suggested population for the particular techniques. These will be generally categorized as: adult, child, individual, group, neurotic, and/or psychotic.

5. Related elements: a listing of some related levels of organization from other areas discussed in the chapter. [3]

10 BASIC PRINCIPLES

The 10 basic principles which will be mentioned here are reminders which will hopefully afford the reader a perspective from which to view the following breakdown of Dance-Movement Therapy areas of concern:

1. Dance-Movement Therapy facilitates more adaptive movement in an individual from the "inside out" not from the "outside in." It is poor reasoning to assume that if an individual does not utilize a particular movement pattern which he needs to live adaptively, that the therapist can "teach it" to him.

2. Work from what you see; never superimpose a movement pattern. This is really another way of saying the first principle. Its foundation is based upon a major goal in therapy which is to broaden and enlarge the existing movement repertoire of an individual rather than trying to affix non-idiosyncratic ways of functioning onto his personality.

3. Always remember the particular environment from which

[2] The principles which Erikson utilizes in development apply here:
  "(1) Each critical item of psychosocial strength discussed here is systematically related to all others, and they all depend on the proper development in the proper sequence of each item; and
  (2) Each item exists in some form before its critical time normally arrives."
  Erik Erikson, Childhood and Society (New York: W.W. Norton & Co., 1963), p. 271.

[3] Although some of the concepts will not have been previously mentioned, they will be discussed by the end of the chapter. This section was put in only for the therapist or student who intends to use this book as a manual, as its rationale only becomes clear when the reader has read through the chapter at least once. If for example, a client is having difficulty with a particular area, the therapist may make use of related elements to assist the individual in the organization of the component in question.

the individual comes as well as if he is to adapt to a new surroundings. For example, to suggest that an American Indian exhibits pathological behavior because he only makes use of directional shape and not shaping as well shows an ignorance which is inexcusable if a therapist is to work with an individual from that culture.

4. Awareness of the qualities and combinations of attributes which are characteristic of an individual can be a vital and useful tool when working toward the organization of a particular pattern. For example, if a person utilizes directness with slowness and it is desirable to move him into a more aggressive pattern, you might utilize this combination and evolve the person into a press: directness, slowness, and strength and gradually as the person becomes comfortable with the addition of this new element of strength, evolve the slowness into acceleration.

5. Awareness of the sequence of a characteristic pattern can also be of importance when working with an individual. If, for example, within the use of tension flow rhythms (which will be discussed in depth later on in the chapter) an individual continually utilizes a particular sequential pattern to work himself up to appropriate expression of anger: (that of oral, oral aggressive, anal sadistic, urethral sadistic, to that of phallic sadistic); the therapist may then make use of this sequence to facilitate the person's experiencing more phallic ballistic patterns.

6. Use of level related components can facilitate organization of a particular element, for example, utilizing related attributes of effort with shape. If an individual has difficulty moving with strength and if a descending pattern is used by him, make use of descending in shaping to aid in the organization of strength.

7. There is always more than one way to aid an individual in the organization of a component. What is best for one may be unsuccessful for another. For example within the use of metaphor alone there are several alternatives, such as concrete images, as be a bull, sensory images, as with music, or abstract images as with expressions of feeling.

8. Remember always that there are levels of organization. To work on kinesthetic discrimination when an individual is unable to respond to any stimulation of this type is fruitless.

9. Generally a therapist can be most assured that an individual has fully organized a particular pattern when he is

able to take that pattern throughout his body with his breathing in direct correspondence to the expression, affording an uninterrupted flow of movement.

10. When feasible it is both expedient and beneficial to make an explicit contract, which determines goals and processes, between therapist and patient(s). It is expedient to the extent that both patient(s) and therapist know where they are going; and it is beneficial to the extent that the patient(s) shares the responsibility with the therapist, responsibility being one of the primary goals of the therapeutic relationship.

FLOW OF BREATH

The most basic of all areas in diagnosis and treatment in Dance and Movement Therapy is the flow of the individual's breathing. It is basic in many ways—first because it is one of the primary indicators of life. From the first scream of breath of the infant to the last gasp of a dying man, the respiratory-circulatory system is the most vital to the physical sustaining and well-being of an individual. Secondly, it is one of the most fundamental behavioral reactions to emotion. Anxiety, anger, sadness are all demonstrated in the rate, depth, and facility of breathing. Thirdly, because of the above two factors, it is usually thought of as one of the major agents in assisting the client toward more adaptive functioning.

In Thus Speaks the Body, Christensen writes:

"Sucking, biting, chewing, micturition, defecation, orgasm, fear and anger, laughter and grief may all be considered as basic organismic responses, responses having an innate biological source. They are all closely related to respiration. In fact, they may be considered so closely related that unless they become integrated with respiration their expression will neither be complete nor give full release and satiation." (p. 75)

Christensen feels through his experience and study of related research that without the integration and coordination with breathing these so-called organismic responses cannot be learned nor fully organized.

The flow of breath is also considered to be the initiating impulse to the individual's interaction with the environment (both internal and external). Symmetrical shape flow as it is referred to by Lamb and Kestenberg, is characterized by the growing and shrinking of the body during normal breathing. Dr. Kestenberg states: "The rhythm of 'shrinking and growing' provides the motor apparatus for the continuous rhythmic transformation of the narcissistic libido into object libido and vice versa."[4]

[4] Judith Kestenberg, M.D., The Role of Movement Patterns in Development (New York: Dance Notation Bureau), p. 88.

Seen in another light, shape flow becomes a basic behavioral reaction to the world outside which corresponds to general feelings of well-being (growing-inhalation) or malaise (shrinking-exhalation).

Breath Flow

This area is characterized by the ability to establish total body flow. This occurs when the whole body is allowed to participate actively in the respiratory process. To understand this concept, one must first define normal breathing. Healthy breathing occurs only if the inspiratory and expiratory processes are both complete. Inspiration commences with an outward abdominal movement brought about by the contraction of the diaphragm and the relaxation of the abdominal muscles. This is then followed in a rhythmic fashion by the upward and outward movement of the thorax. In expiration, the reversal of this wave-like rhythmical flow occurs; the chest relaxes, followed by the diaphragm, and then by the abdomen. This flow is primarily felt in the torso and secondarily throughout the whole body. Once this rhythmical flow is achieved at its normal pace, the movement of the individual will become integrated (Lowen). Organization of the ability to put breathing into the preferred sequence for the desired movement will also be considered here, i.e., breathing must be in the service of movement and expression.

Related Maladaptive Behavior with Suggested Methods and Techniques for Dance-Movement Therapy: Flow of Breath

A. Maladaptive Behavior: Breathing which is blocked, sporadic, inhibited, or increased to a high anxious rate due to another approaching individual. Fear of another's intrusion or potential demands, projected fantasy that if another would get close enough she would find out how "bad and worthless" he (the client) really is, and/or detect a tremendous repressed rage are a few of the possible rationales for this behavior.

Dance-Movement Therapy Techniques:

1. Approach the patient on a diagonal walking in a slow uninterrupted rhythm.

2. With the same flow used in the movement toward the patient, sit quietly beside him as close as possible without disturbing his proxemic "close space" and imposing a threat on him (Hall).

3. The posture and mood of the patient must be duplicated in order to be at his level of communication. In this

way the person feels that no demands are made on him; he is allowed to be where he feels most comfortable.

4. At the appropriate time which may be after several minutes or several sessions depending on the pathology of the client and the abilities of the therapist, other forms of communication can begin.

Several methods of communication have proven successful. Flexibility of choice as well as the knowledge of what the most comfortable method is for the therapist himself are two aspects which must be taken into consideration. One method consists of having the therapist verbally or non-verbally offer his hand to the individual. While holding it in a supportive but non-clutching manner, he may begin to rock the hand of the individual gradually including the whole body in the rhythmic flow process (Chace). Utilizing music which reflects the mood of the relationship with a tempo which simulates that of the breath pulse is often a good idea.[5] Depending on the tactile defensiveness of the individual, the therapist may offer the patient the support of his arms and body in the rocking process.

Once this initial relationship has been established, it becomes a foundation upon which recapitulation of normal developmental organizations and adaptations can take place. Beth Kalish, dance therapist writes, "Following a long period of resistance to any contact, Laura (an autistic child) would go limp and melt into my body as if fused. This seemed to be a physical manifestation of a symbolic relationship. Slowly, over many months, this can change so that the child and therapist can sit and move together as two separate bodies." Janet Adler Boettiger talked of a similar progression in her film on Dance Therapy, Looking for Me.

The type of approach discussed in this section was evolved by Marian Chace the founder of Dance Therapy. It was utilized primarily with psychotic individuals, but it has relevance for all ages and all people.

B. Maladaptive Behavior: The unadaptive blocking or immobilization of the chest, diaphragm, abdomen, or pelvis during the breathing process. This then effects the respiration. The blockage usually occurs through the tensing of various muscles in the torso. An example might be tension in the shoulders or upper back which can inhibit the natural reciprccal swing of the arms when walking. The person looks as if he is literally "scared stiff" to "let go." Some psychological interpretations of tension will be given in the

---

[5] Music by Erik Staie as well as recorded sounds of the ocean tide have proven successful in this area.

chapter on the "Somatatization of Symbols."[6] Another form of blockage, although not as common, is the rendering of the muscles into a flaccid, limp state. The torso is usually lifeless, hollowed, and shortened.

Dance-Movement Therapy Techniques:

1. Movement activities involving the stretching and opening of the chest cavity. For example, hook arms with the individual back to back while standing and bend forward lifting him on your back while pulling his arms away from his chest letting them hang over head in a relaxed manner. (Lowen) (See figure III, #1 p. 19) Or ask the client to yawn and stretch like a cat arching his

Figure III-1. Over the Back Stretch.

[6] Whenever muscles appear to be in a continuous contracted or flaccid state, a possible neuro-muscular pathological etiology must be checked out. There are as many physical pathologic causes (e.g. cerebral palsey, Parkinson's disease, cerebral vascular accident, muscular distrophy, etc.) as there are psychological reasons.

back, extending his legs, loosening and dropping his jaw, and literally "ballooning" himself to occupy the most space possible. [7] (All categories)

2. Movement activities involving the exaggeration of the tense area which is blocking the flow of breathing. This is done in order to produce a safe anxiety state, one in which the individual can become aware of the emotional conflict which has somatatized itself in body tensions, be able to express the emotion he was in conflict about experiencing, and thus bring it into conscious awareness. [8] For example, a young man was not allowing the normal breath pattern of growing and shrinking to occur in his back. His muscles in his upper back were contracted and tense. I suggested to him to exaggerate the tense area, outline and shape it precisely, and then to describe what he was feeling. First, he said it was like a screw digging into his back; he then thought again and said that it was someone's finger jabbing into him. It was his father's who has always pushed him to do more, be better. The tension was released by a "get off my back" exercise (reciprocal elbow jabs to back). (Neurotic, individual, adults)

3. Movement activity which allows the patient to cathect the repressed feelings which are producing tensions in his body and inhibiting his breathing process. This will produce emotions such as anger, sadness, fear, and/or joy. This can be done by, for example, evolving the individual into a free flow movement pattern. The therapist may start with swings or any rhythmic pattern in which there is no intention toward any particular dynamics. Then he looks for any possible change of exertion that might be evolving in the patterns of the person. The client may pick up the tempos of the swings or give them more direction than before or incorporate more strength. The therapist may then encourage this pattern either verbally or by duplicating it himself. He will help the individual to heighten the motor expression of the feeling (in this case anger) as well as help the person to level off the response when appropriate. This can be done, for example, by gradually moving toward indirectness in space, lightness in force, and/or deceleration. (See section on effort for more discussion.) (All categories)

[7] Frederick Perls, M.D., Ralph Hefferline, Ph.D., Paul Goodman, Ph.D., Gestalt Therapy (New York: Dell & Co., 1957), p. 134.
[8] Ibid., p. 287.

4. Movement patterns involving the placement of an individual in various body positions which produce tensions facilitating involuntary movement flow such as those suggested by bioenergists. For example, have the client stand with his feet roughly twelve inches apart while toeing inward. Ask him to bend his knees, lean back, and place his hands at his lower back. (See figure III, #2, below) When the muscles have fatigued sufficiently in this position, the opposing muscle groups will start to coarcate producing a vibratory undulating rhythm throughout the body. [9] (Neurotics, individuals)

5. Movement activities which involve symbolic imagery as catalysts for movement flow. For example, ask the group to become trees, blades of grass, or flowers moving in the wind. Being swimming fishes or bouncing rag dolls can also be suggested. (All categories)

Figure III-2.

C. Maladaptive Behavior: Unnatural breathing patterns such as:

1. Incomplete breath flow pattern. (The therapist can

[9] Alexander Lowen, M.D., The Betrayal of the Body (New York: The MacMillan Co., 1967).

easily see whether or not the belly is moving due to the displacement of the diaphragm or if the chest cavity is lengthening, bulging, and/or widening during inhalation)

2. Lack of adaptive regular even rhythm to the breath flow: for example, if a person is holding his breath during the inhalation or exhalation process or if his flow and/or rate are sporadic.

Dance-Movement Therapy Techniques:

1. Movement activities which stress the breathing process. These are patterns which have a reciprocal in-out, up-down, growing-shrinking sequence. (It is often necessary to remind a person to breath fully and openly no matter what area is being emphasized.)

    a. For example, have the individual lie down on the floor or sit in a chair if the floor is too threatening, and suggest to him to grow, opening his body when he inhales and shrink, closing himself when he exhales. (All categories)

    b. Another way is to have the clients in a group pair up holding each other's hands with one seated and one standing. Then instruct them to move in a reciprocal up-down see-saw pattern, i.e., the person standing pulls the seated person (who is inhaling) up to a standing position while he (exhaling) drops to a seated position. (Bartenieff) (All categories)

2. Movement patterns which stress regularity of breath flow. For example, the therapist might make use of a record with an even repetitive beat to which a group could alternate a breath flow pattern. (Choose a record which allows for the desired rate of breathing) (All categories)

3. Movement activities which involve breathing imagery: such as, suggesting to the group to be balloons which blow up and deflate. For exhalation a child could become a melting snowman, for inhalation—a blossoming flower. The therapist should make sure that they inhale and exhale at the appropriate times. (All categories, especially children)

D. Maladaptive Behavior: Unnatural speech. For example, someone whose speech is shallow or soft or who is unable to raise his voice.

Dance-Movement Therapy Techniques: Use of vocalization when moving.

a. For example, suggest to a group to make non-sensical sounds which might express how they are feeling at the moment. It is easiest to go around a circle at first, giving each person time to make a sound with the contract being that when they feel comfortable, they can respond directly to the sounds that are made. Eventually the whole group then joins in. (All categories)

b. An orchestra of sounds can be created while people move to their own "music." (All categories)

c. In individual sessions, clients are sometimes asked, "If your movements could talk, what would they say?" For example, a young woman with whom I was working was getting in touch with some angry feelings as she slashed and punched at a cushion. With the above cue, she started yelling, "Bitch, bitch! Go to hell! You never came, never!" Prior to this incident, she had no idea that the anger she was releasing each session was due to a deep seated conflict due to her mother's inability to meet her needs as a child. Because of this awareness, she was able to deal with the cause of her rage, better understand her mother, and her relationship with others. (Adult, neurotic)

EFFORT-SHAPE LEVELS OF ORGANIZATION

The concepts of effort-shape as devised by Rudolf Laban and Warren Lamb are used to describe and analyze the quality of human movement. When subdivided into the appropriate developmental lines effort-shape becomes an invaluable tool in Movement Therapy.

Effort can be defined as the way in which kinetic energy is expended in space, force and time. Within this area, pre-efforts demonstrate the degree of defensiveness of an individual and are utilized in the motor expression of ego defense mechanisms. Efforts serve to subdue and control the flow of tension (discussed in Tension Flow rhythms). They are the adaptive patterns by which the ego controls basic drives, such as nurturance, elimination, and sexual gratification. Kestenberg states that the ego translates the id will (tension flow rhythms) into actions (efforts).

Shape is defined as the form of the movement or how the body changes and moves through space as it adapts to the environment (both human and non-human objects). Directional or Dimensional shape is the arc-like or spoke-like bridge between self and objects while shaping is the three-dimensional system which adds complexity and subtlety to relationships. The flow of shape (shape

23

flow) relates to the differentiation of the self from the object. The qualities of growing and shrinking contribute to the motor apparatus for the discharge of libidinal and aggressive energy from the self to the other which affects the transformation of the narcissistic libido to the object libido. (Kestenberg)

In general effort-shape is the way in which a person (1) copes with his inner vibrations and (2) makes adaptations in response to the environment (Bartenieff).

Although effort and shape have been divided into separate subchapters, they are nevertheless bound together. A brief summary of their relationship will be given at the end of the analysis. [10, 11]

Effort Levels of Organization[12]

1. Tension Flow[13]

   This involves the capacity for tension flow which is based on the relationship between the contraction of agonist and antagonist muscles. This flow is either bound (greater participation of antagonists) or free (greater participation of agonists). All rhythms of tension flow can be obtained at birth; however, due to possible lack of physiological maturation and/or environmental stimuli, organization may not yet be achieved. Thus, the flow is unstabilized and not yet organized to a particular zone.

2. Primal Regulation of Tension Flow

   The primal regulation of tension flow involves the ability to distinguish between continuity and discontinuity of motility. It requires the ability to initiate, continue, and cessate basic reflexive movement patterns such as sucking and grasping.

3. Spatial Pre-effort

   This involves the ability to cope with the external forces of space using changes in tension. This requires the ability to change one's mental state to respond to the environment either by channeling movement which is accomplished by the use of even flow tension and/or by moving with flexibility which is achieved by adjusting the flow of tension.

[10] See Appendix for a paralleling of Effort-Shape, Piaget, and Gesell.

[11] See: Cecily Dell, A Primer for Movement Description (New York: Dance Notation Bureau, 1970), for further description of Effort-Shape concepts as well as use of the notational system.

[12] Developmental studies of effort-shape carried out by Dr. Judith Kestenberg. It's application to Dance-Movement Therapy is that of the author.

[13] Although tension flow is not by definition an effort quality, it is nevertheless so closely linked with the efforts that it must be considered here. See also Warren Lamb, Management Behavior (New York: International Universities Press, 1969).

4. Gravitational or Weight Pre-effort

This involves the ability to cope with the external forces of gravity using changes in tension. This requires the ability to change one's mental state to respond to the environment either by moving with vehemence which is accomplished by the use of a high intensity of tension and/or by moving with gentleness which is accomplished by the use of a low intensity of tension.

5. Time Pre-effort

This involves the ability to cope with the external forces of time using changes in tension. This requires the ability to change one's mental state to respond to the environment either by moving with suddenness which is accomplished by the use of a steep ascent of tension and/or by moving with hesitation which is accomplished by the use of a gradual descent of tension.

6. Spatial Effort

This involves the habitual and automatic adaptive pattern which is utilized to cope with the spatial factors of the environment. This requires the ability to utilize indirect movement in which spatial attention consists of overlapping shifts in the body among a number of foci and direct movement in which spatial attention in the body is a pinpointed single focus (Dell). These efforts relate to the capacity to investigate and define (Lamb, Ramsden). With the organization of this level comes the ability to attend to a situation. This pattern, like all of the following efforts, extends to fine as well as gross movements.

7. Gravitational or Weight Effort

This involves the habitual and automatic adaptive pattern which is utilized to cope with weight factors in the environment. This level of organization requires the ability to increase pressure of body weight to a forceful degree entailing the use of strength and the ability to withhold and rarefy the feeling of weight entailing the use of lightness (Dell). These qualities correspond with the capacity to persist with determination to have commitment and conviction (Lamb, Ramsden). With the organization of this level comes the ability to discipline with firmness or sensitivity in intention. [14]

---

[14] Ibid.

25

8. Time Effort

This involves the habitual and automatic adaptive pattern which is utilized to cope with the temporal factors in the environment. This level of organization requires the ability to move with urgency or quickening in time in acceleration and the ability to move prolonging or stretching time out ever so slowly in deceleration. Being able to decide with a sense of timing as well as the capacity to carry-out a task is associated with these dynamics (Lamb, Ramsden). With the organization of this pattern, comes the ability to make a decision on a commitment. [15]

9. Incomplete Efforts and Inner Attitudes[16]

This involves the ability to combine two elements of either space, weight, time, or flow to produce an incomplete effort. This form of organization reveals "inner states of mind" or inner attitudes. The possible combinations are:

a. Weight and flow—"dreamlike, creative or doubting restrictive"

  1. strength and bound—"cramped with tension"

  2. strength and free—"firm, 'easy' flow"

  3. lightness and bound—"delicate, with great care"

  4. lightness and free—"flying, buoyant"

b. Space and flow—"remote"

  1. directness and bound—"controlled"

  2. directness and free—"fluent, channelled"

  3. indirectness and bound—"knotting"

  4. indirectness and free—"undulating"

c. Time and flow—"adaptability, mobility"

  1. sudden and bound—"jerky"

  2. sudden and free—"bouncy, urgent"

  3. sustained and bound—"cautious"

  4. sustained and free—"unharried, lazy"

d. Space and time—"awake"

  1. directness and sudden—"sharp, tapping"

  2. directness and sustained—"smooth"

[15] Ibid.

[16] Abstracted from Marian North, Personality Assessment Through Movement (London: MacDonald & Evans, Ltd., 1972), pp. 246-255.

3. indirectness and sudden—"fluttering"

4. indirectness and sustained —"slow twisting"

e. Weight and time—earthiness

1. strength and sudden—"forceful, energetic"

2. strength and sustained—"powerful, perseverance"

3. lightness and sudden—"lively, delicate"

4. lightness and sustained—"peaceful, soothing"

f. Weight and space—stability

1. strength and directness—"firm, commanding"

2. strength and indirectness—"sinuous, striving"

3. lightness and directness—"gently pointed"

4. lightness and indirectness—"sensitive"

10. Externalized Drives

This involves the ability of the individual to automatically combine three elements involving the attributes of space, weight, time, and/or flow in order to cope with the total environment. This requires the appropriate body-movement organization for:

a. Action—flowless

1. light, slow, indirect—float

2. light, quick, direct—dab

3. light, slow, direct—glide

4. light, quick, indirect—flick

5. strong, quick, direct—punch

6. strong, quick, indirect—slash

7. strong, slow, direct—press

8. strong, slow, indirect—wring

b. Passion—spaceless[17]

1. strong, quick, bound—"possessive, aggressive"

2. strong, quick, free—"uncontrolled, wild"

3. strong, slow, bound—"restrictive"

4. strong, quick, free—"outgoing, powerful ease"

5. light, quick, bound—"little irritations"

[17] Ibid., pp. 263-266.

27

6. light, quick, free—"flippant"

7. light, slow, bound—"hesitant, shy"

8. light, slow, free—"indulging, formless"

c. Vision—weightless

1. direct, quick, bound—"penetrating"

2. direct, quick, free—"lively reactions"

3. direct, slow, bound—"slow penetration of restricted idea"

4. direct, slow, free—"continued pursuance of clear aim"

5. indirect, quick, bound—"controlled sudden avoidance"

6. indirect, quick, free—"sudden imaginative ideas"

7. indirect, slow, bound—"cautious"

8. indirect, slow, free—"imaginative indulging"

d. Spell—timeless

1. direct, strong, bound—"concentration"

2. direct, strong, free—"resolute drive for power"

3. direct, light, bound—"tentative, meticulous"

4. direct, light, free—"clear direction"

5. indirect, strong, bound—"restricted"

6. indirect, strong, free—"generous, influencing"

7. indirect, light, bound—"uncertain restraint"

8. indirect, light, free—"yielding to influence"

Related Maladaptive Behavior with Suggested Methods and Techniques for Dance-Movement Therapy

1. Tension Flow

Maladaptive Behavior:[18] Predominence of neutral flow throughout the body such that there is little or no reversal from free to bound flow or vice versa.

---

[18] It is important to remember when viewing so-called maladaptive behavior that absence of movement elements are not necessarily pathological. Their absence may facilitate an individual's functioning at a particular job or in a cultural environment. Behavior becomes maladaptive only when the person cannot satisfy his own needs and meet the demands of the environment. Therefore the behavior that will be discussed must always be considered along with the cultural-socio-economic profile of the individual.

Dance-Movement Therapy Techniques:

1. Movement activities which involve an evolutionary development of flow fluctuations (free-bound alternation). Depending on the patient, movement can flow from proximal to distal, cephalo to caudal, from the center of gravity-out or the reverse. Whichever is the most basic and/or least threatening are to be centered on first.

   For example some severely regressed schizophrenic individuals seem only to allow movement to occur on a distal, i.e., only lower arms and lower leg, level. The therapist may then take this cue and suggest to the patient to move these parts in a rhythmic flow pattern. He may then gradually suggest to him to involve the more proximal parts of the body.

   On other occasions the individual must first get a sense of the center of gravity via such basic patterns as sitting, standing, being on "all-fours," or tilting himself and regaining balance. Once this awareness has developed he may then feel more comfortable rocking in a flow pattern alternating his center stance (Bartenieff) (All categories).

2. Movement activities involving the development of involuntary coarcation of muscles (Lowen). This quick abrupt change from free to bound flow can then be exaggerated to produce flow throughout the body.

   For example, suggest to the person to stand in a parallel position, his legs roughly eight inches apart, and his knees bent to produce roughly a 130° angle. Due to muscle fatigue, the upper leg muscles' [agonists (quadraceps) and antagonists (hamstrings)] holding contractions will become more pronounced producing a shaking motion. Suggest to the person to take this rhythm into his whole body (Neurotic, adults, individual, groups).

3. Movement activities involving the use of imagery. For example instruct the group to become a giggling motor (children).

   Related elements which will be discussed in later chapters are the utilization of enactive, iconic, or abstract cognition, [19] one to one or parallel group, [20]

---

[19] Will be discussed in detail in the Cognitive Representation Levels of Organization.
[20] Will be discussed in detail in the Primary Group Levels of Organization.

use of egocentric or object-dependent relationship with therapist, [21] and use of symmetrical shape flow. [22]

2. Primal Regulation of Tension Flow

A. Maladaptive Behavior: Difficulty in distinguishing between preserving and establishing movement flow.

Dance-Movement Therapy Techniques:

Suggest to the person to move and to cease movement. Use of graded sensory reinforcements may be required.

For example, have the person sit or stand in front of a mirror (visual cue), touch his arm and ask him to move it (tactile cue and verbal cue). You may wish also to weight the arm or body part. The same procedure may be used when asking the person to stop moving. The extra stimuli may be reduced when the individual is ready (All categories including retarded individuals, usually not applicable to neurotics).

B. Maladaptive Behavior: Difficulty in adaptively initiating, continuing and cessating basic movement patterns.

Dance-Movement Therapy Techniques:

Movement activities which facilitate the starting and stopping of patterns.

For example, instruct the person to walk. The therapist may assist him by taking his arms and gently pulling him. Then suggest dropping on the floor, gently draw the person down to the floor with the therapist and hold the position.

Reinforcement can be done through the use of such games as "freeze" i.e., the group is allowed to move until the therapist instructs them to freeze at which time they hold their position (children, individual, groups, neurotic, psychotic, perceptual-motor impaired).

Related elements which will be discussed later are one-to-one, parallel group, object ambivalent or semi-autonomous relationship with therapist, and the use of symmetrical shape flow.

3. Spacial Pre-effort

A. Maladaptive Behavior: Difficulty in adaptively coping with the external forces of space through appropriate

---

[21] Will be discussed in detail in the Dyadic Levels of Organization.
[22] Will be discussed in detail in the Shape Levels of Organization.

30

channeling. This is a person for example, who has difficulty restricting himself to one thing at a time. He cannot get the appropriate mental feeling about moving in an even manner in space.

Dance-Movement Therapy Techniques:

1. Movement activities involving a conscious effort to maintain even flow in moving through space. The therapist can assist this process by reminding the person to channel his body and by keeping him centered on his mental attitude rather than the accent being on the environment. She might say, for example, "keep thinking about how you should be and move while you are channeling; your thoughts and whole body are narrowed toward this one movement." (All categories)

2. Movement activity in which the person reinforces channeling by a verbal stream of consciousness centering on the appropriate mental attitude for this pattern. The therapist instructs the person to relate to her as he is thinking during the exercise. He might say, "I am zeroing in, all my feelings are pin pointed in, my body is like a line, I feel restricted," etc. (All categories)

B. Maladaptive Behavior: Difficulty in coping with the external forces of space through appropriate flexibility. This might be an individual who is over-cautious or who is restraining when he should be more able to adjust himself.

Dance-Movement Therapy Techniques:

Movement activities involving a conscious adjustment of flow of tension in moving through space.

For example, the therapist keeps suggesting to the person to think about being more flexible when moving in space, to indulge himself, to allow himself to take in as much space as possible. His own verbal cues may also help. (All categories with change of vocabulary)

Related elements are: one-to-one, parallel group, object ambivalent or semi-autonomous relationship with therapist, use of horizontal directional shape.

4. Gravitational or Weight Pre-effort

Maladaptive Behavior: Difficulty in coping with the external forces of weight through the appropriate use of vehemence and/or gentleness. This might be a person who maladaptively overuses gentleness to the extent that he becomes too vague or who overuses vehemence such that he feels cramped and static all the time.

Dance-Movement Therapy Techniques:

1. Movement activities involving a conscious effort to maintain high-intensity flow and/or low-intensity flow.

   As with the space pre-effort the therapist gives verbal cues to the individual to move with gentleness and/or vehemence. (All categories)

2. Patterns involving alternation of these two qualities might also assist the individual in sufficiently polarizing these patterns. (All categories)

   Related elements are: one-to-one, parallel groups, object ambivalent or semi-autonomous relationship with therapist, use of vertical directional shape.

5. Time Pre-effort

Maladaptive Behavior: Difficulty in adaptively coping with the external forces of time through the appropriate use of suddenness and/or hesitation. This state might be exemplified by a woman who has difficulty evolving her mental state from hypnotic dreaminess into conscious use of steep ascent of tension or gradual descent of tension.

Dance-Movement Therapy Techniques:

1. Movement activities involving a conscious effort to maintain suddenness and/or hesitation. The therapist gives verbal cues. (All categories)

2. Patterns involving alternation of these two qualities.

   For example, involve the person in consciously feeling a slow deliberateness of movement juxtaposed with one in which he readies his state for quick sudden patterns. The therapist may wish to have the person sense the difference without moving followed by taking this movement into space. (All categories)

   Related elements are: one-to-one, parallel group, object-ambivalent or semi-autonomous relationship with therapist, use of sagittal directional shape.

6. Spacial Effort

   A. Maladaptive Behavior: Difficulty in moving with directness when adaptively appropriate. This could manifest itself in an individual who had an exaggerated predominant use of indirectness. The person would lack a

32

focus, be all over the place without any real purpose, and would have a great deal of difficulty sticking to any task.

Dance-Movement Therapy Techniques:

Gross and fine movement patterns involving the use of directness. It is useful when working with efforts to utilize imagery or to create an actual environment which requires the person to make use of the particular dynamic, in this case directness.

For example, the therapist could suggest to a group that there is a very narrow bridge over some water in front of them and for them to walk across being careful not to fall off. (All categories)

The use of the balance board is sometimes effective.

Related element: Use of narrowing shaping.

B. Maladaptive Behavior: Difficulty in moving with indirectness when adaptively appropriate. A person might be too narrow and meticulous, unable to take in the full range of space.

Dance-Movement Therapy Techniques:

Gross and fine movement patterns involving the use of indirectness.

For example, suggest to the individual that there is a field of flowers in front of her and that she wants to take in all of them and that not being in any hurry she can indulge this desire. (All categories)

Or through the use of an obstacle course of objects which keep a person from going straight to the other side of the room, but rather permit him to move through space in a meandering pattern could be used. (All categories)

Related elements: Use of widening shaping plus object ambivalent or semi-autonomous relationship, and parallel or task group.

7. Gravitational of Weight Effort

A. Maladaptive Behavior: Difficulty in moving with strength when adaptively appropriate. A person with this problem might be over-sensitive, lacking in the feeling of having his feet on the ground, and demonstrate very little drive.

33

Dance-Movement Therapy Techniques:

The engagement of the person in moving with strength in gross and fine movements.

Such as, the therapist might suggest that the person walk at his own pace, and utilizing the time and space element with which the client feels most comfortable, suggest to him to take a firmer step perhaps using the imagery of stamping out.

Related element: Sinking in shaping.

B. Maladaptive Behavior: Difficulty in moving with lightness when adaptively appropriate. This could be a person who used an excessive amount of strength with little or no rebound into lightness. He would be stubborn to the point of being cramped and immobile; he would be aggressively dogmatic.

Dance-Movement Therapy Techniques:

Movement activities involving the use of lightness in gross and fine patterns.

The person might be taken through fantasy of having a huge weight on him being lifted off his shoulders while he is moving at his own pace about the room.

(Stress the incorporation of as many qualities within his existing repertoire as possible. For example if this individual always makes use of directness with strength, combine the directness with the experiences in lightness as well.) (All categories)

Related elements: Use of rising shaping as well as parallel or task groups, semi-autonomous, object-ambivalent relationship.

8. Time Effort Stage

A. Maladaptive Behavior: Difficulty in accelerating when adaptively appropriate. This person might be very slow in making decisions wanting to cling to what has existed in the past.

Dance-Movement Therapy Techniques:

Movement activity involving the use of acceleration in gross and fine movements.

For example, throw a ball to the individual and suggest to him its "a hot potato" and for him to quickly throw it back. Or suggest to a group that they might dart and stop here and there throughout the room as if they were birds escaping from a net. (All categories)

Or the therapist might make use of the attributes of space, force, and/or flow to provide a comfortable base for acceleration. The increase in tempo can be gradual such as with the theme from Zorba the Greek or much quicker such as with a change of a song.

Related element: Use of retreating in shaping.

B. Maladaptive Behavior: Difficulty in decelerating when adaptively appropriate. For example, someone might be unable to slow down such that he is over-hasty about decisions and demonstrates reckless behavior.

Dance-Movement Therapy Techniques:

Movement activity involving the use of deceleration in gross and fine movement.

The therapist might have the group move in an atmosphere filled with glue or underwater, or suggest to a person that he slowly go up to the sleeping monster and then jump on him (children). (All categories)

Related elements: Use of advancing in shaping plus parallel or task groups, object-ambivalent or semi-autonomous relationship with therapist.

9. Incomplete Efforts and Inner Attitudes

A. Maladaptive Behavior: Difficulty in utilizing a two-effort quality when adaptively appropriate.

Dance-Movement Therapy Techniques:

1. Movement activity which makes use of existing repertoire of inner attitudes to evolve the individual toward organization of the two-effort pattern desired.

For example, supposing the therapist senses that the person was lacking in a feeling of stability (weight and space), and that she seemed to always be in a far off remote state (space and flow). The therapist could then utilize her pre-existing organization of space and if her disposition in flow was free, gradually evolve her into a straightforward (directness) sensitivity (lightness) which produces a gentle steadfastness. Once this is a comfortable state, the therapist may wish to evolve her into a more solid pattern through evolution into strength with directness. (All categories)

2. Movement activities which involve forms of dancing which are related to the incomplete efforts. For example, the therapist might suggest African music such as the <u>Misa Luba</u> or Olatungi to get in touch with weight-time factors, where as space-flow, its opposite, fits more into classical ballet. Weight-space is more characteristic of the American Indian dances.[23] (All categories when ready)

3. Movement-drama activities which call for the dancing out of an attitude, image or many attitudes through the use of an appropriate plot or poem. (All categories, with children use only concrete images.)

   For example, suggest concepts such as exuberance (strength-free flow), dogmatic (strength-suddenness) or carefree (indirect-free) or images such as a fluttering butterfly (quick-indirect) or a prowling panther (strength-flexibility).

B. Maladaptive Behavior: Unadaptive exaggeration of a two-effort inner attitude.[24]

   Such as:

   a. Weight and flow

      1. strength and bound—"obsessional, fixated, nightmarish"

      2. strength and free—"overbearing, reckless"

      3. lightness and bound—"oversensitive, overcautious"

      4. lightness and free—"unfocused drifting"

   b. Space and flow

      1. directness and bound—"withdrawing, very narrow view of problem"

      2. directness and free—"overemotional, without caution"

      3. indirectness and bound—"gets cramped trying to cope with too many aspects at once"

      4. indirectness and free—"can't stick to the point, attention swamped by feelings"

---

[23] North, <u>Ibid.</u>
[24] Ibid.

c. Time and flow

1. quick and bound—"hasty jump to conclusion, inhibited"

2. quick and free—"rushing at decision"

3. slow and bound—"cramped"

4. slow and free—"excessively sentimental"

d. Space and time

1. direct and quick—"narrow-minded"

2. direct and slow—"clinging to limited view"

3. indirect and quick—"agitated, anxious"

4. indirect and slow—"vague, lazy"

e. Weight and time

1. strength and quickness—"domineering, impatient"

2. strength and slowness—"boring insistence"

3. lightness and quickness—"fleeting intention"

4. lightness and slowness—"can't come to grips with self"

f. Weight and space

1. strength and directness—"stubborn, unimaginative"

2. strength and indirectness—"grinding, always changing focus"

3. lightness and directness—"superficial, attention to the little detail"

4. lightness and indirectness—"butterfly mind, meandering"

Dance-Movement Therapy Techniques:

Movement patterns involving the gradual evolvement away from the exaggerated degree by movement toward the use of the reciprocal quality.

For example, if a person over-uses boundness coupled with directness; it will manifest itself in a controlled over-cautiousness which might result in, or be a part of a withdrawal reaction. Maintaining the directness the boundness is gradually relaxed through the involvement in direct-free patterns. Upbeats and rebounds into free before and after a direct-bound pattern will also assist in

37

releasing him from the continuous use of this pattern. (All categories)

Related elements: Use of corresponding shape affinities, parallel or task group, semi-autonomous or chumship relationship.

10. Externalized Drives

Maladaptive Behavior: Difficulty in utilizing a 3-effort combination when adaptively appropriate. For example, a young woman who has trouble expressing her anger is unable to combine directness, strength, and acceleration to produce a punch. The closest she would come to it would be a bound, indirect, accelerated gesture.

Dance-Movement Therapy Techniques:

1. Movement activities which evolve the group or individual from one externalized drive into another.

For example, if the woman discussed above were to work with a dance therapist, he might suggest to her either verbally, showing her and/or taking her through the pattern, to evolve the indirectness to directness producing a quick, direct, bound pattern. The boundness might then be relaxed more into free-bound alternation at which time the therapist might carefully introduce strength to produce the action of punching. (All categories)

Quite often when a person is frightened of the heightened aggressive expression of a punch, a press (strong, direct, and sustained) might be introduced as less threatening. The therapist might suggest to the person to press against his palms as he presses against the client's.

2. Movement activities which make use of imagery such as flicking off water (light, indirect, quick) or slashing wood in two with a sword (strong, indirect, quick) or floating along with a cloud having all the time in the world (light, sustained, indirect) (all categories).

3. Movement activities involving gradually or quickly evolving the whole body into an externalized drive.

Such as suggest to a group to flick off imaginary water with the hands, then whole arms, arms and shoulders, then upper torso, etc. (All categories)
Sometimes it is more effective to quickly involve a client into a full effort sequence. An example of this phenomenon is a situation in which a catatonic schizo-

Punch

Wring

Press

Slash

Figure III-3. Fighting Efforts.

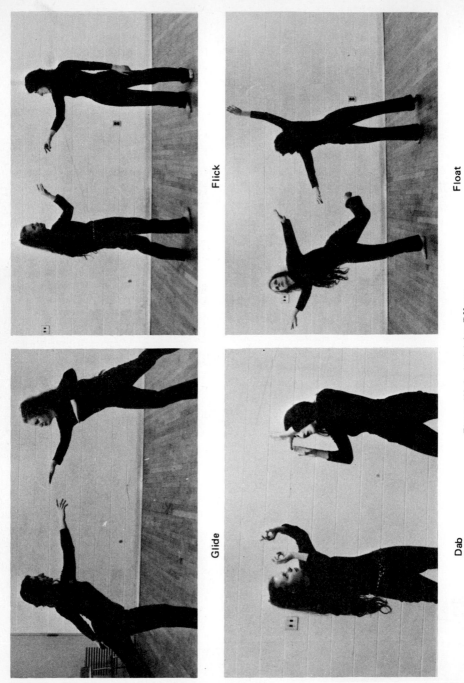

Flick

Float

Glide

Dab

Figure III-4. Indulging Efforts.

40

phrenic was sliding into a split. The therapist instructed him to "stamp your feet!" (use of a punch: strong, quick, direct, full effort) He immediately got out of his static state and began vigorously stamping. (Following this session, he began talking for the first time since his stay at the day hospital.) (Catatonic psychotic individuals)

Related elements: Use of all related shape combinations; task, egocentric, and/or cooperative groups; semi-autonomous, chumship or autonomous relationship with the therapist.

SHAPE LEVELS OF ORGANIZATION[25]

1. Symmetrical Shape Flow

This involves the capacity for spontaneous symmetrical shape flow which is based on the alternation of growing and shrinking of the body in bipolar form. Shape flow is part of the congenital motor equipment which eventually is used by the individual in his attempts to relate to the atmosphere. In affinities, shape flow is characterized by a transition from free flow extensor dominance to bound flow flexor dominance. In general, when an individual grows in shape, body boundaries subside and the feeling is one of expansiveness, generosity, pride, pleasure, and satiation—of wanting to take in the environment. Conversely when an individual shrinks and closes himself from the environment the feeling is associated with need such as hunger, pain, despair, as well as retreat from the surroundings. The person may feel himself to be small, empty, or insignificant as compared to what is around him.

Shape flow must occur in three dimensions in order for it to be considered fully organized.

Width—widening (expanding, taking in) narrowing (constricting)

Height—lengthening (extending, elongating) shortening (becoming smaller)

Depth—bulging (feeling full) hollowing (feeling empty)

2. Asymmetrical Shape Flow

This involves the capacity for asymmetrical changes in shape which are based on the alternation of growing and

[25] Concepts formulated by Kestenberg.

41

shrinking of the body in unipolar or asymmetrical form. With this apparatus, the individual is able to react to discrete stimuli and to discriminate between what is satisfying and what is repulsive. He is also capable of relating to the space inside his body as well as that which is outside in his immediate near space. Relatedness to external objects is more specified and delineated via "channels" for tension flow rhythms. This adaptive pattern serves secondary narcissism.

In order for this ability to be considered fully organized, the individual must have in his repertoire all the following shape components:

Widening into and out of

Narrowing into and out of

Lengthening up and down

Shortening up and down

Bulging forward and backward

Hollowing forward and backward

3. Horizontal Dimensional Shape

This involves the capacity of automatic spoke-like or arc-like shaping of the body in space in the horizontal direction. At this level the body or parts of the body is (are) capable of expanding horizontally sideways and across the body in response to the environment and its objects. This ability is related to the pre-effort stage of channeling and being flexible and is in dominance during the oral phase.

4. Vertical Dimensional Shape

This involves the capacity for automatic spoke-like or arc-like shaping of the body in space through the vertical dimension. At this level, the body or body parts is (are) capable of extending vertically upwards and downwards in response to the environment and its objects. This ability is related to the pre-effort stage of gentleness and vehemence and is in dominance during the anal phase.

5. Sagittal Dimensional Shape

This involves the capacity for automatic spoke-like or arc-like shaping of the body in space in the sagittal dimension. At this level, the body or body parts is (are) capable of protruding forwards and backwards in response to the environment and its objects. This ability is related to the pre-effort stage of hesitation and suddenness and is in dominance during the urethral phase.

42

6. Horizontal Shaping

This involves the capacity for automatic shaping of the body in space utilizing the horizontal plane. This is accomplished by projecting the body or body parts in a spreading and enclosing shaping of space. These qualities are associated with the ability to explore the shape of possibilities within a given situation and when matched with the effort spatial affinities demonstrate an ability to establish and maintain reciprocal communication (Lamb, Ramsden).

7. Vertical Shaping

This involves the capacity for automatic shaping of the body in space utilizing the vertical plane. This is accomplished by projecting the body or body parts in an ascending and descending shaping of space. This is the plane of confrontation and intention. The effort affinities are lightness and strength and when appropriately combined with corresponding qualities in shaping result in the ability to present self and others and to influence and persuade while maintaining a sense of confidence.

8. Sagittal Shaping

This involves the capacity for automatic shaping of the body in space utilizing the sagittal plane. This is accomplished by projecting the body or body parts in an advancing and retreating shaping of space. This is the plane of anticipation and farsightedness and involves the ability to be committed. When combined with the effort affinities of slowness and quickness, the capacity to carry out plans or "operate" is manifested (Lamb, Ramsden).

9. Combination of Two Qualities in Shaping

This requires the ability to combine shaping automatically in two planes to cope with either the communicational-presentational, communicational-operational, or operational-presentational situations in the environment.

10. Combination of Three Qualities in Shaping

This involves the ability of the individual to automatically combine three elements in shaping involving aspects necessary for communication, presentation, and operation in order to cope with the spatial environment. It must be remembered that transition from one plane to another requires a shaping movement involving three spatial tendencies. At this level the individual must be able not only to move peripherally but also transversally (movement which passes between the body center and periphery) as well as centrally (movement which passes through the center of the body).

At this point shape flow is seen as being in total service of shaping[26] in creating the inner as well as outer shape.

Related Maladaptive Behavior With Suggested Methods and Techniques for Dance-Movement Therapy

1. Symmetrical Shape Flow

A. Maladaptive Behavior: Difficulty in adaptive usage of symmetrical shape flow in any of the three dimensions. What is quite characteristic of many individuals who wish to withdraw from reality is a predominately fixed position comprised of solely narrowing, shortening, and hollowing. Minimal breathing occurs so as not to disturb this body attitude.

Dance-Movement Therapy Techniques:

1. Appropriate movement activities of the flow of breath area. See pp. 18-22; for example: Those techniques utilized to promote normal breath flow.

2. Movement activities which stress work on the separate elements of shape flow with the idea of combining them once the person has organized them. For example, suggest to the person to lie down on a mat or floor. If he uses primarily space efforts or horizontal shape, the therapist may wish to first work on the widening and narrowing of the body during the breath flow, i.e., having the client widen when inhaling and narrow when exhaling. If the client needs more help in understanding and organizing this process, the therapist may wish to use a mirror, show the person her own body, touch the area to be worked on pressing during exhalation, asking the person to "breathe into my hands" or "breathe into the direction of my hands" during inhalation, or move various body parts. (All categories)

3. Dance activities which make use of atmospheric imagery. Such as "It's a beautiful day. You are very much alive and filled with joy. Take in your surroundings." (All categories)

[26] Shaping in movement involves the changing of three dimensional relationships of the body to space and objects. Kinesthetically, shaping requires flexion or extension, abduction or adduction, and internal or external rotation. Shape flow must be able to be in the control of the individual so as to be put into the preferred sequence for the desired movement, e.g., when an individual spreads his body, he might also wish to widen in shaping.

44

B. Maladaptive Behavior: Difficulty in relating to the inner space of the body. For example, an individual, who has literally "stuffed" feelings that he was unwilling to express into his gut area may because of his previous desire to lose awareness of them, maintain a contracted state in that area.

Dance-Movement Therapy Techniques:

Movement activities involving continuous breathing into area while lengthening, widening, and bulging followed by the expelling of the feelings during the exhalation process (Lowen). For example, the man mentioned above would be instructed (if he is ready to work with the repressed feelings) to breath into his gut and to allow himself to release the tightness in that area. The therapist would remind him to let himself feel as much as he is ready. He may wish to talk about the experience and the feelings it brought up, this talking process often assists the individual in integrating the experience and resolving conflictual issues.[27] (Adults, neurotic, individual)

Related elements: Flow of breath; enactive level of cognition; one-to-one or parallel group; egocentric, object dependent, or object-ambivalent relationship with therapist.

2. Asymmetrical Shape Flow

A. Maladaptive Behavior: Difficulty in the adaptive usage of asymmetrical shape flow in any of the dimensions. For example a child may not have fully organized the ability to grow asymmetrically toward a positive stimulus.

Dance-Movement Therapy Techniques:

1. Movement activities which promote individual reaction to discrete stimuli in various areas of the individual's kinesphere.

For example with the use of imagery, the therapist might say to the child that he is glued on to the floor and can't move his feet or his arms and that he is to respond to a magic magnet which draws his body to it.

---

[27] There are those, such as Dr. Judith Kestenberg who are strongly against Dance-Movement Therapists helping the client through verbalization feeling that talking and moving should not be combined. Others, like myself feel if the client deems it necessary, that it should not be curtailed. It is vital also to note here that a therapist should never use the suggestion of "breathing into an area" before he has worked on releasing some of the muscle tension in the blocked part. Not doing so may cause serious damage and at best dizziness from inexperience with the increased amount of oxygen.

The therapist then walks around the child stressing areas for him to lengthen up, widen into etc., as the magnet draws near. (All categories)

2. Movement activities which involve discrimination between attractive and repulsive stimuli. For example, the individual could still be "glued," however; this time the therapist makes use of two stimuli, one positive to be approached and one negative to be withdrawn from. She might have the child pick two puppets to personify the characteristics (children).

B. Maladaptive Behavior: A continuous maladaptive asymmetrical body stance.

Dance-Movement Therapy Techniques:

Movement activities which promote normal symmetrical flow of breath through the use of various cues. For example:

a. Use of touch: The therapist alternates pressing and releasing the contracted shrunken side in the rhythm of the person's flow of breath.

b. Use of pre-efforts and efforts: For example, use of lightness to release a shortening down to a lengthening upward or strength to release a shortening up to a lengthening downward.

c. Use of efforts with flow: For example, suggest that the person make use of bound strength in the asymmetrically shrunken area to be released into free strength after a period of time.

d. Use of sound: For example, suggest to the person to increase the bound flow in the area followed by a sound producing release. (All categories)

Related elements: Enactive and iconic levels of cognition, primal regulation of tension flow; object-ambivalent relationship with therapist; one-to-one, or parallel group.

3. Horizontal Dimensional Shape[28]

Maladaptive Behavior: Difficulty in adaptively moving in an arc-like or spoke-like manner in the horizontal.

---

[28] Blind children need experience with forwards and sideways direction, deaf children with sideways and backward direction.

Dance-Movement Therapy Techniques:

Movement activities involving the horizontal direction stressing shaping sideways and across the body.

This is often carried out through the use of location of objects in space. For example, reaching out in a spoke-like manner to grasp an object or a hand. (All categories)

Related elements: Enactive and iconic levels of cognition, space pre-efforts, object-ambivalent or semi-autonomous relationship with the therapist. One to one, parallel, or task group.

4. Vertical Dimensional Shape

A. Maladaptive Behavior: Difficulty in adaptively moving in an arc-like or spoke-like manner in the vertical.

Dance-Movement Therapy Techniques:

Movement activities involving the vertical direction stressing shaping upward and downward. For example suggest that the group become something; such as, a machine that has up and down moving parts. (All categories)

B. Maladaptive Behavior: Difficulty in maintaining weight constancy.

Dance-Movement Therapy Techniques:

Activities which assist the individual in being aware of and adaptively utilizing his center of gravity.

Here, as in many of the areas, it is often best not to cloud the difficulty through the use of imagery. For some, getting in touch with how the weight changes from, for example; a seated to a standing position is where the therapist should begin. (All categories)

Related elements: Enactive and iconic levels of cognition, object-ambivalent or semi-autonomous relationship; one-to-one, parallel, or task group; use of weight pre-effort.

5. Sagittal Dimensional Shape

Maladaptive Behavior: Difficulty in adaptively moving in an arc-like or spoke-like manner in the sagittal direction.

47

Dance-Movement Therapy Techniques:

Movement activities involving the sagittal direction stressing shaping forward and backward.

These can be as simple as moving a circular group into the center and back out again. (All categories)

Related elements: Enactive and iconic levels; object-ambivalent or semi-autonomous relationship; use of time pre-efforts, one-to-one, parallel, or task group.

6. Horizontal Shaping

A. Maladaptive Behavior: Difficulty in adaptively shaping in the horizontal plane either by spreading and/or enclosing: such as, an individual who continually turns people away with scattering gestures when internally he desperately longs for closeness.

Dance-Movement Therapy Techniques:

1. Movement activities involving general use of spreading and enclosing patterns.

For example suggest to a group in a circle that in the center there are all the things they want, have them gather them up and hold them close to themselves. (All categories)

2. Activities which make use of objects to help facilitate the organization of this level.

Such as the utilization of sheets of material for capes. If it is a child's group, the therapist might suggest that they become villains showing them how to hold on to the edge of the cape and spread it open and closed such that only their eyes peer out. (All categories)

B. Maladaptive Behavior: Difficulty in adaptively exploring all the possibilities when attending to a situation. For example, someone who can only see his side of the situation.

Dance-Movement Therapy Techniques:

Movement activities which involve the exploration of the space around the person (real or imaginary). For example, create an environment which requires the moving of certain objects in space to find a particular object or person. (All categories)

Related elements: Use of spatial efforts, parallel or task group, object-ambivalent, or semi-autonomous relationship with the therapist.

7. Vertical Shaping

   A. Maladaptive Behavior: Difficulty in adaptively shaping in the vertical plane either by rising or sinking. For example, an individual might always "sink" into oblivion when he is asked to "rise" to the occasion as with the meeting of new people or the involvement in other novel situations.

   Dance-Movement Therapy Techniques:

   Movement activities involving the use of rising and sinking patterns.

   Such as, suggest to a group of children that they are rising in an escalator (have them start in a squat position), or have them pretend to be flowers who are asleep who rise upwards and outwards toward the sun (a held light) and who sink back down at nighttime (all categories with changes of imagery).

   B. Maladaptive Behavior: Difficulty in adaptively presenting himself. For example, someone who has difficulty standing on his own two feet due to poor self-esteem.

   Dance-Movement Therapy Techniques:

   Movement activities involving the presentation of self in various situations.

   For example, have a group wander amongst each other and whenever they pass someone suggest to them to stand up tall and "snub" the person. (All categories)

   Or, the therapist may wish to use imagery; such as, having a person play the proud matador with another being the bull. (All categories)

   Related elements: Use of weight efforts; parallel or task group; object ambivalent or semi-autonomous relationship with the therapist.

8. Sagittal Shaping

   A. Maladaptive Behavior: Difficulty in adaptively shaping in the sagittal plane either through advancing and/or retreating. For example, someone who maintains a retreating pattern for every situation.

   Dance-Movement Therapy Techniques:

   Movement activities involving the use of advancing and retreating.

   For example, suggest to a group of children to slowly

49

advance toward a haunted house and when they arrive to quickly retreat. Be sure to have everyone start low and rise as they move forward reversing the response during the retreat. (All categories)

B. Maladaptive Behavior: Difficulty in the operation of tasks when adaptively necessary. For example, a man might be able to think out what to do in situations but be unable to ever carry any of his ideas out.

Dance-Movement Therapy Techniques:

Movement activities involving the carrying out of an activity through various forms of locomotion. For example, have the person anticipate what is to come in a real or imaginary drama and have him act on his decision. If he has a tendency toward acceleration work on retreating patterns first, with a tendency toward deceleration-advancing patterns.

Related elements: Use of time efforts, parallel or task group, object ambivalent or semi-autonomous therapeutic relationship.

9. Combination of Two Qualities in Shaping

Maladaptive Behavior: Difficulty in adaptively combining two qualities in shaping either aspects of vertical and horizontal planes, vertical and sagittal planes, or horizontal and sagittal planes.

Dance-Movement Therapy Techniques:

Movement activities involving the use of combining the various patterns of two shapes in space.

Such as alternating enclosing and sinking with spreading and rising within the person's own timing. (All categories when age appropriate)

Related elements: Use of inner attitude affinities, parallel or task group, semi-autonomous or chumship relationship.

10. Combination of Three Qualities in Shaping

A. Maladaptive Behavior: Difficulty in adaptively combining three qualities in shaping. For example, an adolescent might have problems in reforming his identity and may be helped by learning to combine shape qualities in the relating to the environment.

Dance-Movement Therapy Techniques:

Movement activities which involve the combining of three shape qualities in space.

For example, as with the 2-shape suggestion, alternate patterns of enclosing, sinking, and retreating with spreading, rising, and advancing toward an object in space. (All categories)

B. Maladaptive Behavior: Difficulty in adaptively shaping in a peripheral, transverse, and/or central pattern. Schizophrenic individuals will quite often lack central or transverse patterning. Their movements are only on the periphery as many are threatened by involvement of the self with the environment.

Dance-Movement Therapy Techniques:

Movement activities which involve peripheral, transverse, and/or central patterns in shaping.

For example, if an individual has difficulty utilizing more central shaping, the therapist might commence where the individual is most comfortable, i.e., if predominant combination within his repertoire is retreating, sinking, and enclosing, suggest to him to start the movement in his torso as if hit in the stomach (all categories with change in imagery).

Related elements: Use of related externalized drives; parallel, task, egocentric and cooperative group; semi-autonomous, chumship, or autonomous relationship with therapist.

Interrelationship Between Effort and Shape

Integration of the Effort-Shape components will be more effective if they are taught jointly. Since each effort has its corresponding shape, both elements will act toward reinforcing each other. If an individual exhibits a preponderance of efforts over shape, he will appear to be aloof; he may possess adequate drives but no ability to direct his need satisfaction to the appropriate object in the environment. He may have a somewhat functioning ego but he would be bereft of the capacity to relate to others.

Conversely, if the individual demonstrates far more shaping than efforts, his relationship to his environment will lack feeling and energy, like a "walking zombie," he would move affectlessly through his daily existence.

With regard to the use efforts: The gain expense ratio or the relationship between the amount of flow changes (from free to bound or bound to free) as versus efforts attributes (i. e. , light, strong, quick, etc.) utilized in each effort component or single movement demonstrates the degree to which affect is differentiated and rigid or spontaneous. For example; two times as many attributes as flow changes shows an individual lacking in spontaneity whereas six times as many flow changes to attributes depicts a child-like personality (Kestenberg).

The load factor (Kestenberg) another concept, measures the complexity of movement in the average amount of effort attributes used in each component. This computation seems to correlate with I. Q. as well as with emotional pathology; 33% would be seen as low; 55% as high.

It should also be noted that a high discrepancy between space efforts and horizontal shaping, weight efforts and vertical shaping, and/or time efforts and sagittal shaping is indicative of conflict behavior (Kestenberg, Lamb). If effort is matched with shape skills in communication, presentation of self and ideas, and the carrying out of one's life, the individual will probably be on a more functioning level (Lamb). This functioning correspondence also invites interaction with others in the area which is being exhibited (Ramsden). For example, if an individual talking with another utilizes spatial efforts with appropriate horizontal shaping in the communicational sphere, the other person will be more readily able to attended to and receive a clear message, thus facilitating his response. If on the other hand, using directness, he continuously tilts his torso forward and back, gesturing in the vertical plane, the other may feel that he is not that interested or involved in truly sharing with him what he feels nor interested in his response. The other person has picked up a certain inconsistency in the individual's behavior, thus what is responded to often becomes unclear.

EFFORT	SHAPE
Tension Flow	Shape Flow Design
Flow adjustment	Looping, undulent
Even intensity	Linear
Low intensity	Low amplitude
High intensity	High amplitude
Gradual increase in intensity	Soft reversal
Steep increase in intensity.	Angular reversal

Widening

Enclosing

Ascending

Descending

Advancing

Retreating

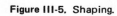

Figure III-5. Shaping.

53

Pre-effort	Directional Shape
Flexible	Sideways
Channeled	Across the body
Gentle	Upward
Vehement	Downward
Hesitation	Forward
Sudden	Backward

Effort	Shaping
Indirect	Spreading
Direct	Enclosing
Light	Ascending
Strong	Descending
Deceleration	Advancing
Acceleration	Retreating

EFFORT   SHAPE

Flow	
Free	Growing
Bound	Shrinking

POSTURE-GESTURE LEVELS OF ORGANIZATION

Among the behavioral phenomena which may be utilized as an indicator of developmental adaptive organization in movement, is the use of posture and gesture. These two concepts were developed by Warren Lamb and have been enlarged upon in his work as a management consultant.

Gesture is defined simply as action which is confined to one or more parts of the body without encompassing the whole body.

Posture is action involving a continuous adjustment of every part of the body with consistency in the process of variation. [29] When this occurs, the motion possesses a coordination of flow or tone throughout.

Clearly both postural and gestural movement are needed to adequately adapt to the environment. Although observations of

[29] Warren Lamb, Posture and Gesture (London: Gerald Duckworth & Co., 1965), p. 16.

54

individual posture-gesture patterns demonstrate that there are idiosyncratic ranges, it is generally felt that the more a person can enlarge his repertoire, especially where posture and gesture are seen to overlap, the more he is said to be acting in accordance with his real self. [30]

Based on the study of current findings, Christensen formulated some propositions concerning the importance of postural movement. Among them are the following:

1. The release of basis organismic response presupposes a postural basis.

2. Their release can be interfered with by a dissolution of their postural basis, and

3. The permanent dissolution of the postural basis for an organismic response will have repercussions on the organism's breathing pattern. (Page 75)

Thus in order for motoric behavior utilized in emotional expression and basic need gratification to be fully organized and integrated, it must involve a full postural merger with the appropriate flow of breath.

Posture-Gesture Levels of Organization

1. Posture-Gesture Flow

This involves the capacity for tension and shape flow variation utilizing both postural and gestural movement.

2. Merging of Gesture Systems

The merging of gesture systems involves the ability to link any effort or shape quality with another so that one attribute merges into another within a gestural sequence. [31]

3. Merging of Posture-Gesture Systems

The merging of P-G systems involves the ability to link posture with gesture while maintaining consistent shaping and/or efforts. Gestural shaping and/or efforts may be "backed up" by postural movement which is consistent in quality with the gesture, or posture may be "carried on" by gesture (Lamb). [32] In either case one must evolve and

---

[30] Ibid., p. 85. It is important to note here that within certain contexts naturally gesture is more appropriate than a G-P or P-G merger. For example, for a Dance-Movement Therapist to utilize a P-G merger when greeting a schizophrenic individual for the first time would be quite inappropriate. (A schizophrenic generally moves using only peripheral gestures. If the therapist greeted him with a postural movement, he would not be meeting the person at his level of communication.)

[31] For example, an arm raised upwards in a light upbeat flowing into an arc-like forward quick, direct motion.

[32] Lamb, op. cit., p. 37.

flow from the other. All attributes of effort, i.e., those adapting to space, weight, and time as well as those qualities of shape, must be able to be utilized in posture-gesture merging in order for this level to be fully organized.

Related Maladaptive Behavior With Suggested
Methods and Techniques for
Dance-Movement Therapy

1. Posture-Gesture Flow

A. Maladaptive Behavior: The difficulty in adaptively varying tension and/or shape flow with postural movements; for example, an individual might be suppressing sexual needs due to guilt or anxiety which manifests itself in a blocked pelvic area.

Dance-Movement Therapy Techniques:

Movement activities which involve the use of tension and/or shape flow with postural movements. Such as, the therapist might first ascertain which aspects of flow a woman prefers within her gestural repertoire. She might, for example, move a great deal utilizing the adjustment of tension flow with a corresponding undulent, looping quality in shape flow. The therapist could then suggest to her a postural pattern such as one involving opening and closing using these qualities. (All categories)

B. Maladaptive Behavior: The difficulty in adaptively merging posture with gesture in tension and/or shape flow. This could show itself in a tense individual who has been unable to merge his gestural strivings into postural adjustment.

Dance-Movement Therapy Techniques:

1. Movement activity encompassing changes of flow involving evolution from gestural to postural patterns and from postural to gestural. For example, a pattern which makes use of breathing as a rhythmic force in the flow of gestural (the chest and diaphragm) to postural movement (the whole body).

2. Movement activities which involve asymmetrical or unipolar shape flow; for example, the person initially responds asymmetrically in a gesture to a stimulus.

56

This may take the form of an initial unipolar widening or narrowing, lengthening or shortening, and/or bulging or hollowing followed successively by the whole body. (All categories)

Related elements: One-to-one or parallel group. Egocentric, or object ambivalent relationship with therapist.

2. Merging of Gesture Systems

Maladaptive Behavior: Difficulty in adaptively merging gesture systems in effort and/or shape. Autistic children often have bizarre unrelated gestures involving ritualistic repetitive mannerisms.

Dance-Movement Therapy Techniques:

Movement patterns involving the linking of various effort attributes of space, weight, and time and/or shape attributes of communication, presentation, and operation as well as the combination of effort-shape affinities in merging gestural systems.

Here again, the therapist may wish to make use of the person's preferred efforts and/or shapes. It also is of help to make use of related tension and/or shape flow attributes to evolve the person into the corresponding efforts and/or shapes:

Tension Flow	evolve to	Effort
Flow adjustment	"	indirectness
Even intensity	"	directness
Low intensity	"	lightness
High intensity	"	strength
Gradual increase in intensity	"	slowness
Steep increase in intensity	"	quickness

Shape Flow Design	evolve to	Shaping
Looping, undulent	"	spreading
Linear	"	enclosing
Low amplitude	"	ascending

57

Shape Flow Design	evolve to	Shaping
High amplitude	"	descending
Soft reversal	"	advancing
Angular reversal	"	retreating

(All categories)

Related elements: One-to-one, or parallel group, object-ambivalent or semi-autonomous relationship with therapist.

3. Merging of Posture-Gesture Systems

A. Maladaptive Behavior: Difficulty in adaptively linking gesture with posture and/or posture with gesture while maintaining any consistent shaping and/or efforts. A person in which P-G merger was not present might take on a doll-like or puppet-like quality in his movement. [33] His repertoire would have an artificial quality due to the lack of postural adjustment.

Dance-Movement Therapy Techniques:

1. Movement patterns which involve the linking of a posture with a gesture or vice versa while maintaining consistent shaping and/or efforts.

Such as:

Posture-gesture merging activities which have indirect application to daily tasks with which the individual or individuals have difficulty.

For example:

1. Analyze the appropriate effort-shape P-G merging for a key point in a daily task of the individual.

2. Have the individual fully integrate this pattern so that his original limited movement (usually solely gestural in nature) is extended.

3. Have the individual apply this pattern to the appropriate activity or activities. [34] (Adults, individual, neurotic)

2. Movement activities which utilize real or imaginary sports activities which stress P-G mergers. Such as the pitching of a baseball. (All categories)

B. Maladaptive Behavior: Unadaptive extraneous move-

[33] Lamb, ibid., pp. 31-32.
[34] Ibid., p. 171.

58

ment patterns utilized in lieu of a natural signature of posture-gesture overlap. [35] For example, if an individual had much unmerged posture, it might demonstrate "a lack of cultivation, either skill training, education generally, or social development." [36]

Dance-Movement Therapy Techniques:

The therapist should not expect to change the example above's way of handling or ordering his physical behavior, that is his personal style of responding to "a lack of cultivation" in a particular area. But what can be done is to increase the client's ability in the area in question in terms of the particular movement repertoire needed to perform the task. If it is a job situation, the therapist might wish to advise the person if his own repertoire is not compatible with what is required (all categories except children).

C. Maladaptive Behavior: Minimal or no adaptive exhibition of emotions on a postural level. This could be the type of person whose so-called expressions of emotion are not really believable. For example, she greets a lover by extending her arms as if to embrace, but when he moves toward her she maintains her torso in a rigid tense manner.

Dance-Movement Therapy Techniques:

1. Movement which involves taking an emotion, expressing it gesturally, and evolving it into a postural form (the more postural an expression of emotion, the more meaningful it is to the individual).

For example, the therapist might start the pattern utilizing the portion of the body most often used in gestures by that person or group, (generally the hands and forearms) and evolve them into an expressive pattern such as strong, quick, indirect-slashes moving first the arms, then shoulders, upper torso, etc. (All categories)

2. Movement activities in which verbalization is incorporated into the pattern "verbal communication backed up by consistent postural movement will be experienced as a convincing and sincere expression of the verbal message." [37]

[35] Ibid., p. 66.
[36] Ibid.
[37] Portion of study carried out by Warren Lamb Associates and presented at the 1971 Dance Notation Bureau Conference in New York.

Merger of Posture-Gesture Flow

Merger of E/S Gesture Systems

60

For example, an individual who is involved with stamping (strong, quick, direct) his leg while merging in repeated vertical postures might yell each time, "I won't!" (All categories)

Related elements: Parallel, task, or egocentric-cooperative group; semi-autonomous or chumship relationship with therapist.

TENSION FLOW RHYTHMS LEVELS OF ORGANIZATION

The importance of the role of rhythm in human development and in the learning of adaptive patterns has generally been acknowledged among both psychologists and educators. Psychotherapists have also observed that rhythm is one of the few basic qualities that is pleasurable to a regressed individual; it is therefore often one of the few avenues of communication open to the therapist. Kestenberg, restating Kris says, "the primitive rhythm of affective discharge as it is modified by the ego becomes a vehicle for non-verbal communication."[38]

Rhythm is one element which is generally present at a Dance-Movement Therapy session; therapists make use of it but quite often only on a superficial basis. Because of its importance to the individual and therefore to the therapeutic process, this tool cannot be overlooked or casually used. Rhythm is especially significant if the individual's primary or only method of communication is on a non-verbal level. Rhythm, because of its major importance, then becomes the basic medium for interaction and therapy. Psychiatrists, psychologists, and other psychotherapists (unless they have studied Dance Therapy) do not have facility with this tool. The knowledgeable movement therapist has, however, and can therefore serve a primary role in the psychotherapy of an individual who could not be worked with using more traditional methods.

This primitive method of communication acts also to integrate the total being. It has been found that when the flow of rhythm involves all the muscle systems, an increased awareness of the total body and sense of well being quite often ensues.

However, a therapist who superimposes his own natural rhythmic pattern or tries to use an alien beat found in some piece of music, rather than first observing the rhythmic level of his client, may produce a negative reaction and serve to further withdraw an already regressed individual.

The rhythms that will be discussed here are those described by Dr. Judith Kestenberg. She states:

"Rhythms of tension-flow serve need satisfaction such as

[38] Judith Kestenberg, M.D., "The Role of Movement Patterns in Development: I. Rhythms of Movement," Psychoanalytic Quarterly, XXXIV (1965), p. 3.

61

sucking, defecating or urinating. With the onset of psychic functioning the tension flow apparatus is used for drive discharge in such a way that oral, anal, urethal and genital drives find their expression in appropriate motor rhythms."[39]

True differentiation and organization are contingent upon these motor channels being established at the appropriate discharge zone.

Tension Flow Rhythm	Need	Motoric Drive Discharge	Discharge Zone
Oral libidinal	Nourishment	Sucking	Mouth
Oral Aggressive	Nourishment	Biting, (teething) Chewing	Mouth
Anal Libidinal	Elimination Defecation	Expelling, twisting	Anal sphincter
Anal Sadistic	Elimination Defecation	Shaping evacuation control Straining, holding, expelling	Anal sphincter
Urethral Libidinal	Elimination Micturition	Flowing, urinating	Bladder, urethra
Urethral Sadistic	Elimination Micturition	Bladder control Running, darting Stopping	Bladder, urethra
Inner Genital	Sexual gratification	Embracing, inclusive floating	Female genitals
Phallic	Sexual gratification	Intruding, ballistic leaping, jumping	Male genitals

When drive discharge is localized, the ego is then able to control and integrate the drive.

These rhythms exist in pure and mixed form in combination with each other. All rhythms when organized should be present in pure form for adaptive functioning. An integrated adult will have an increased ratio of mixed rhythms to pure (5:1), denoting a higher degree of sublimation, as well as more libidinal rhythms than sadistic in mixed form stressing subtleties of indulging pleasurable need gratification over aggressive-sadistic discharge (Kestenberg).

[39] Judith Kestenberg, H. Marcus, E. Robbins, J. Berlowe, and A. Buelte, "Development of a Young Child as Expressed Through Bodily Movement," unprinted paper. Sands Point, New York, p. 4. It is also important to note here that "Rhythms in shape flow give structure to the changes of tension by providing patterns of interaction with need-satisfying or frustrating stimuli and objects," p. 4.

Tension Flow Rhythms Levels of Organization[40]

1. Oral Libidinal

This level involves the ability to control libidinal oral
rhythms of tension flow which aids in the development of a
primary system of communication. This phase is concomitant with the initial differentiation of the infant from the
primary object, the mother. The oral rhythm can be
described as smooth, repetitive undulations from free to
bound flow which is characterized by sucking. ᴨᴧᴧᴧ
The primary zone for this movement is, of course, the
mouth; however, if an infant is viewed during normal
breast feeding[41] the observer will note that the oral rhythm
may be carried throughout the body. In order for the infant to organize this task he must perceive his initial experience with the environment (via his mouth) as a
pleasant and need satisfying one. It is vital, therefore,
that the mother (his first environment) appropriately mediate his sucking rhythms, neither bulging her breast so
that the infant's control over nursing is totally curtailed,
nor withdrawing it out of anger or fear of rejection.
Mother's body must be soft and somewhat yielding to provide an indulging cushion of tender acceptance. A body
that is bound or flaccid-limp will transmit negative kinesthetic cues and promote an atmosphere of potential anxiety
and mistrust.

2. Oral Aggressive

This involves the ability to control oral sadistic rhythms
of tension flow which serve to aid in the further evolution
of differentiation of the individual from his environment.

The oral aggressive rhythm can be defined as jerky, sharp,
repetitive fluctuations from free to bound flow. This is the
rhythm of biting and chewing. ᴧᴧᴧ ᴧᴧᴧ The rhythm
is first observed in teething when the infant attempts to
work his milk teeth through his gums. As with oral incorporative rhythms, these rhythms may be found in other
areas of the body—particularly in the reaching out and
grasping of objects with the hand.

3. Anal Libidinal

This involves the ability to control anal libidinal rhythms
of tension flow which aid in the adjustment to new positions
and trial actions.

---

[40] Adapted from Kestenberg, ibid.

[41] (Feeding in which the mother's movement patterns do not interfere with those of her
child's.)

This rhythm is characterized as having predominantly low tension with small changes in intensity.

Here the ability to coordinate breathing with defecation as well as to integrate and experience the "letting go modality" as part of the personality are vital (Christensen).

4. Anal Sadistic

This involves the ability to control anal sadistic flow patterns which further serve in presentation and confrontation as well as the awareness of qualities of weight. Independence and more of a sense of autonomy evolves here in the so-called "terrible two's."

This rhythm is defined as having a high intensity of even bound flow with eventual relaxation into a free flow state.

The individual must be able to "maintain high tension while squatting (shortening of body shape) and to lengthen in low tension."[42] Bowel control is present here as well as movements of a holding expelling quality in other parts of the body.

5. Urethral Libidinal

This involves the ability to control urethral libidinal rhythmic tension flow patterns which serve in the operation of tasks and decisions. This is a passive level in which the toddler flows everywhere with limitless time.

This rhythm is characterized by gradual decrease and increase in tension.

6. Urethral Sadistic

This involves the ability to control urethral sadistic rhythmic tension flow patterns which serve in the mastery of locomotion and in the capacity to start and stop suddenly. The developmental physiologic task is that of bladder control.

This rhythm is defined as having sharp reversals from free to bound flow often starting and stopping suddenly.

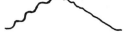

7. Inner Genital Libidinal

This involves the capacity to control inner genital libidinal patterns which serve to aid in the development of receptiv-

42 Ibid., p. 16.

ity. Inclusive, indulging behavior, as well as appropriate sexual identity involving identification with same sex parent or surrogate figure are part of this level of organization. This is generally considered to be primarily a feminine rhythm; however, it has also been observed in the tunica dartos movements of the scrotum. Normal males exhibit these patterns, but not to the extent that it is found in females.

This rhythm is characterized by undulant wavy flat transitions between free and bound flow.

8. Inner Genital Sadistic

This involves the ability to control inner genital sadistic rhythmic flow which serves to aid in the development of orgiastic states and during childbirth.

This rhythm is characterized by large undulant transitions between free and bound flow.

9. Phallic Libidinal

This involves the ability to control phallic libidinal rhythms which is characterized by high intensity rounded flow adjustments with steep increases and decreases in tension.

Intrusive behavior, as well as appropriate sexual identity involving identification with same sex parent or surrogate figure are part of this level of organization.

10. Phallic Sadistic

This involves the ability to control phallic aggressive rhythms which characterize leaps and the ballistic qualities in most sports activities.

It is characterized by high intensity sharp flow adjustment with steep increases and decreases in tension.

11. Phallic-Inner Genital[43]

This involves the ability to combine and control phallic and inner genital rhythms. This P-F rhythm, as it has been named by Marcus and Kestenberg, is the predominating characteristic genital rhythm of normal adults, and is exhibited during coitus.

It is characterized by medium intensity transitions.

Related Maladaptive Behavior With Suggested Methods and Techniques for Dance-Movement Therapy

1. Oral Libidinal

A. Maladaptive Behavior: Difficulty in the utilization of a pure oral libidinal rhythm[44] when adaptively appropriate. For example, a mother may be unable to mediate the sucking rhythm of her infant during feeding. Or an individual might be unable to comfort himself during a sad experience by, for example, a rocking pattern or a gesture involving the stroking of the face or the opposite arm.

Dance-Movement Therapy Techniques:

1. Movement activities involving the control of smooth, repetitive undulations from free to bound flow and from growing to shrinking in shaping. It is generally easiest if the movement evolves from gesture and links onto posture. For example, involve the person in a rocking pattern; such as first holding the person's hand and moving it in a rocking fashion with gradual involvement of the torso and whole body. If the person is seated the therapist may utilize a sagittal rocking pattern to slowly rock him to a standing position. Taking both hands, the clinician may gently sway with the person to the beat of a music which reinforces this rhythmic pattern. (All categories especially schizophrenics and those suffering from withdrawal reactions.)

2. Movement activities involving passive manipulation of the individual by the therapist in an oral rhythm. Such

---

[43] Phallic-feminine rhythm.

[44] Pure rhythms are: oral, oral aggressive, anal, anal sadistic, urethral, urethral aggressive, feminine, feminine sadistic, phallic, phallic sadistic. Examples of mixed rhythms: oral-anal, oral sadistic-phallic, feminine-feminine sadistic, etc. The presence of rhythms in a pure form is adaptively needed in a functioning individual. A normal adult will have mixed rhythms; however if rhythms in their pure form are not present, needed drive investment and differentiation will not occur. (Kestenberg)

as the rocking of an individual. (Psychotic, children, individual) (See Figure III, #6, below.)

Figure III-6. Rocking.

3. Movement activities involving taking in and symbolic receiving, such as the imaginary taking in of a favorite food; (suggestion of sweet foods and fruits might be helpful). (All categories)

4. Movement activities involving patting, and/or rubbing; such as having each person pat-tap his whole body with an even repetitive motion. (All categories)

5. Movement activities which enlarge upon grasp and release patterns. Such as a G-P merger starting with the opening and closing of the hands ending in a grasp (shrinking, bound flow) release (growing, free flow) pattern involving the whole body. (All categories)

6. Use of verbalizations during session; for example, suggest to the individual or group to repeat "yes" with each oral rhythm or ask the group to respond to such questions as "What is your favorite sweet?" (All categories)

B. Maladaptive Behavior: Oral Syndrome: bound deep neck muscles and upper back, torso arched, stiffening and resistance of arm and leg extension, tense jaw (Lowen), perhaps due to a rejecting mother with a bound torso.

Dance-Movement Therapy Techniques:

Movement activities involving getting in touch with the repressed conflicted oral needs through, for example,

67

recalling or restaging infancy by either calling for mother or by providing a negative surrogate parent. Once the individual releases all the bound sadness and anger, then tender and positive feelings may be transmitted to the client via positive mother figures through, for example, a simulated nursing movement drama affording him an opportunity to incorporate loving, accepting feelings and thus become his own good mother.

Related elements: horizontal directional shape, spacial pre-efforts; egocentric relationship with therapist; one-to-one or parallel group; flow of breath; weaning ritual process.

2. Oral Aggressive

A. Maladaptive Behavior: Difficulty adaptively initiating and cessating oral aggressive rhythms. Such as an individual who has difficulty expressing aggression even in its most primitive form.

Dance-Movement Therapy Techniques:

1. Movement activities involving the control of jerky, sharp, repetitive undulations from free to bound flow and from growing to shrinking in shape flow. Such as a dance which emphasizes the maintaining of an accented repetitive beat either by banging the floor with hands or feet, clapping, or use of percussion instruments such as sticks, symbols, drum. (All categories)

2. Utilization of imagery which would stimulate an oral aggressive pattern. Such as being wooden soldiers which move in a jerky manner. (All categories)

3. Movement activities which involve seizing and grasping. For example, have each person seize imaginary desired objects such as people, food, love, etc. in the middle of the circle keeping all of it in their arms. Then each go around to others and try to grasp what they have. (Mutual sharing can also occur here although not component related.) (All categories)

B. Maladaptive Behavior: An individual with a "hanging on bite" exhibited by a tense throat and jaw and chest, as well as fixed, bound glaring eyes. The person may be ambitious and rivalrous and literally spit with anger, or he may be unable to yell out at all.

Dance-Movement Therapy Techniques:

1. Use of movement-imagery which facilitates snarling and biting. Such as the group all being angry lions. (All categories except psychotic)

68

2. Movement activities involving the exaggeration of the tension in the jaw to facilitate relaxation. Such as have the individual bite onto a towel while lying down. The therapist may then pull on the towel lifting the client's head off the mat.

A reciprocal tug of war with a towel or similar article while holding it in the mouth is also successful. (All categories) Use of yelling and other verbalizations which help the individual towards differentiation and in-dividualization, such as asking the patient, "I am me; who are you?" (Chace) A group yell is also helpful as it is often more safe. The group may start with a gentle tone and work up to a roar. (All categories)

Related elements: Horizontal direction, and spacial pre-efforts, one-to-one or parallel group; object de-pendent relationship with therapist; Body-Image: differentiation of the body from the environment.

3. Anal Libidinal

A. Maladaptive Behavior: Difficulty in adaptively utilizing anal libidinal rhythms. This could be an individual who is excessively involved or fixated at the oral aggressive level, i.e., someone who snaps and "bites" at his environment being unable to respond in a more gentle manner.

Dance-Movement Therapy Techniques:

1. Movement activities involving rhythmic control of low tension with small changes in intensity. Such as use of playful games like peek-a-boo or pat-a-cake with the feet. (Children, groups, individual, psychotic, neurotic)

2. Movement which entails brief intervals of holding and releasing or activities involving brief growing out into space and releasing. Such as is found in many ball games. (All categories)

3. Use of ambivalent verbalizations such as "I will, I won't." (All categories)

B. Maladaptive Behavior: Ambivalent, careless, and frus-trated individual characterized by an inability to feel committed often observed moving from leg to leg. In children this often takes the form of constant kicking and slapping; excrements become used as ammunition. This behavior can be caused by "a lack of consideration for the child's rhythm, lack of understanding of his feeling of belonging to his own product." (Christensen)

Use of props or imagery which can involve messing and smearing. Such as an imaginary walk in mud or "foot"-finger painting while dancing. (All categories except, of course, those who have dirt-phobias.)

Related elements: Object ambivalent relationship with therapist, parallel group, use of weight pre-efforts and vertical shape.

4. Anal Sadistic

A. Maladaptive Behavior: Difficulty in adaptively utilizing anal sadistic rhythms. This could be an individual who has a great deal of difficulty standing up for himself, presenting himself in a situation. He may not be able to confront another or to refuse to carry out an offensive order.

Dance-Movement Therapy Techniques:

1. Movement activities involving the rhythmic control of high intensity even bound flow followed by relaxation into a free flow state both in posture and gesture. For example, suggest to the individual to move to a vertical position from lying supine and/or prone or have him move from a seated to a standing position using this rhythmic pattern. (All categories)

2. Movements involving presentation of self as dominant and proud; such as being "the boss" or a peacock. (All categories)

3. Use of negative verbalizations such as "No," "I won't." (All categories)

4. Movements involving taking "No" throughout the body. Suggest, "How many ways can you make your body say 'No'?"—e.g., stamp feet, shake your head, etc. (All categories)

Suggest to the patient to lie on a couch or bed and have him alternately kick his feet and arms while shouting "No!" After a period of time, his head should automatically move from side to side. Any holding back on the part of the patient will be demonstrated by lack of coordination. (Lowen) (See Figure III, #7, p. 71) (Neurotic, adult)

5. Movements involving imaginary throwing, dropping, destroying, shoving, pushing, and wringing; for example, ask the whole group (or individual) to lift a heavy negative imaginary object in the center of the circle. After they have done this, have them throw it away, stamp on it, or whatever they wish. (All categories)

70

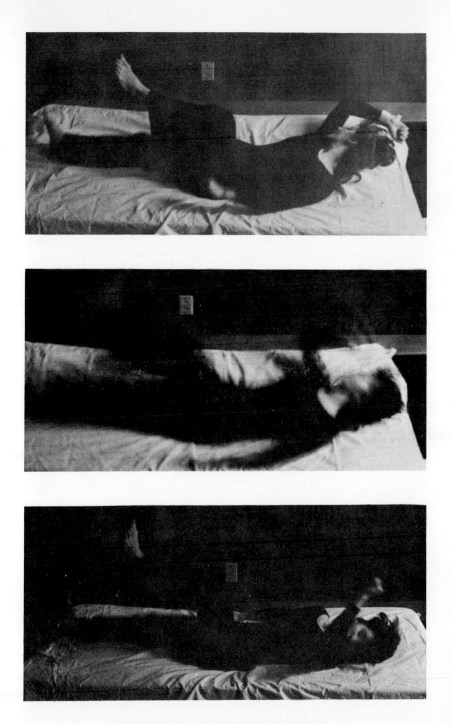

Figure III-7. Talking "No" Through the Body.

71

B. Maladaptive Behavior: Difficulty in completing anal
    sadistic pattern or a straining inward. This is the
    individual who some call the "tight-ass" and, by the
    way, he actually does have a clenched contracted
    buttocks and tense anal sphincter; his thighs and
    calves, too, will be bound. With a forward, upward
    presentational pelvic tilt and a tightening of the shoul-
    ders, the characteristic low backache syndrome ap-
    pears. He may be compulsively meticulous, per-
    fectionistically productive, hostile and determined, but
    generally he will have a great deal of difficulty expres-
    sing anger, keeping it locked up inside a tense body
    structure. This behavioral complex may be due to pre-
    mature parental pressure for bowel control and order-
    liness and/or to authority figures never allowing the
    toddler any independent negative response. Feces often
    become invested with negative affect and the individual
    feels himself to literally be a "piece of shit"—one who
    must keep those "shitty feelings" constipated, bound up
    inside at all costs. (Lowen, Christensen)

Dance-Movement Therapy Techniques:

1. Movement activities which stress the vertical, down-
    ward release of tension. Such as have the individual
    arch the upper part of his back over a grounded stool
    while he is holding on. The person is instructed to
    push down from this somewhat horizontal position to a
    vertical one while exhaling with possible vocalization.
    The finished position is a vertical squat. (See Figure
    III, #8, p. 73 for more detailed description.) This
    pattern is then repeated. (Adult, neurotic)

    Related elements: Use of vertical shape and
    gravitational-weight pre-efforts and efforts, drive-
    object: investment of aggressive drive in external
    objects, semi-autonomous relationship with therapist.
    Parallel group, vestibular perception.

5. Urethral Libidinal

    Maladaptive Behavior: Difficulty in adaptively utilizing
    urethral libidinal rhythms. This could be shown in an
    individual who has difficulty allowing himself to move
    with a relaxed flowing quality, i.e., his movements
    are always stiff and/or jerky. He is unable to take time
    to linger on a subject or with a person, dawdling and
    day-dreaming is definitely out of the question. The eti-
    ology of this behavior could stem from a family situa-
    tion which would curtail the pleasurable flow of an

72

Figure III-8. Vertical Release.

idling child with continuous demands for premature bladder control and/or for temporal structure on his carrying out of activities.

Dance-Movement Therapy Techniques:

1. Movement activities involving rhythmic control of gradual decrease and increase in tension with soft reversals in shape flow. For example, dancing to flowing Hawaiian music. (All categories)

2. Use of imagery of a derivative of urethral libidinal patterns. For example, being a melting snowman or other forms which involve liquid, or wandering through an imaginary environment. (All categories)

3. Water ballet.

   Related elements: Sagittal shape and time efforts, semi-autonomous relationship with therapist, parallel or task group.

6. Urethral Sadistic

   Maladaptive Behavior: Difficulty in adaptively utilizing urethral sadistic patterns. This is someone who cannot start and stop quickly. He may literally be "all over the place" as far as time is concerned and has trouble knowing when he should become operational. Premature bladder control may be another causal factor here resulting in a tense pelvic area and/or constant cystitis. In this case the individual runs everywhere, always "doing" officiously and precisely and never allowing himself to "be."

Dance-Movement Therapy Techniques:

1. Movement activities involving the rhythmic control of sharp reversals from free to bound flow which start and stop suddenly both in postural and gestural patterns. Such as activities involving quick starts and stops of a dashing nature. (All categories)

2. Games involving running then freezing, as well as those which require knowing when the right time is for moving quickly. (All categories)

   Related elements: Sagittal shape and time efforts, locomotor activities, semi-autonomous relationship with therapist, parallel or task group.

7. Inner-Genital Libidinal

   Maladaptive Behavior: Difficulty in the adaptive use of

feminine rhythms; for example, a woman who never appropriately identified with a same-sex object for what ever reason may not utilize this pattern within her usual repertoire.

Dance-Movement Therapy Techniques:

1. Movement activities involving the rhythmic control of undulant flat wavy transitions between free and bound flow both in postural and gestural patterns. For example, movement activities of a floating nature (light, indirect, slow) or a dreamy state (lightness and free flow). (All categories)

2. Utilization of imagery or objects which would stimulate the quality such as the use of a flowing cape or sheet with slow waltz-like balletic music. (See Figure III, #9, p. 75) (All categories)

Figure III-9.

Related elements: Use of lightness, indirectness, and slowness in effort and related shape, same sex female group. Chumship relationship with the therapist, puberty ritual process.

8. Inner-Genital Sadistic

Maladaptive Behavior: Difficulty in the adaptive use of feminine sadistic rhythms. For example, a woman who has difficulty facilitating delivery due to inappropriate use of movement during labor.

Dance-Movement Therapy Techniques:

1. Movement activities involving the rhythmic control of

large undulant transitions between free and bound flow in posture and gesture. For example, movements of an expulsive nature (female).

2. Use of related imagery; such as of delivery (female).

Related elements: Task group, chumship relationship with therapist, puberty ritual process.

9. Phallic Libidinal

Maladaptive Behavior: Difficulty in the adaptive usage of phallic libidinal rhythms. This might be characterized by a male who has not yet resolved the oediple crisis, i.e., who has not yet formed a proper identification with a male figure or who has a highly smothering and/or seductive mother.

Dance-Movement Therapy Techniques:

1. Movement activities involving the rhythmic control of rounded flow adjustments with steep increases and decreases in tension. Such as movements involving penetration through an imaginary atmosphere. (All categories)

2. Movement activities of an exhibiting and/or controlling nature. Such as have each person in the group move to the center of a circle and dance alone for a period of time, e.g., "Telling us something he wants to say with his body," while the others watch. (All categories)

Related elements: Chumship relationship with therapist, task group, puberty ritual process.

10. Phallic Sadistic

Maladaptive Behavior: Difficulty in the adaptive use of phallic sadistic patterns. Such as a person who is unable to express his anger on other than a primitive level, e.g., instead of punching he bites and spits (OS).

Dance-Movement Therapy Techniques:

1. Movements involving the rhythmic control of high intensity sharp flow reversal with steep increases and decreases in tension in both posture and gesture. For example, movements involving jumping, leaping, and driving. (All categories)

2. Movements of a sharply aggressive nature (but not biting). For example, punches or use of every sports activity which utilizes ballistic patterns. (All categories)

76

Related elements: Chumship relationship with therapist, task group, Drive-object: investment of aggressive drive in external objects, use of strong, quick, direct efforts and related shape, puberty ritual process.

11. Phallic Inner Genital

Maladaptive Behavior: Difficulty in adaptive use of adult rhythms. This is an adult who for whatever reason has not yet evolved into a genital level of functioning. Mature sexual behavior will be difficult for him.

Dance-Movement Therapy Techniques:

1. Movement activities involving the combination of phallic and feminine inner genital rhythms producing medium intensity reversals. Such as those patterns found in everyday adult, interactional behavior. (All categories except children)

2. Movement patterns involving the central pelvic initiation of this pattern with a postural merger. For example, dancing to Afro-Carribean music. (All categories except children)

Related elements: Autonomous relationship with therapist, cooperative ego-centric group, all effort-shape combinations, marriage ritual process.

DYADIC INTERACTION LEVELS OF ORGANIZATION

Probably the most important element of the therapeutic process is the relationship established between the therapist and his patient. The success of the organization of many of the adaptive patterns is contingent upon this dyadic relationship. If a rapport of trust, understanding, and respect has not been constructed; it will adversely effect the total movement activity. Therefore, it is imperative that the dance therapist comprehend not only the level and needs of the individual but those of himself as well. The therapist's own needs of dependency, competition and aggression must be satisfied outside the therapeutic relationship. Countertransference[45] is contra-indicated here, as it is in most areas of therapy.

Factors Which May Originally Have Caused
Maladaptive Behavior in This Area

A neonate's normal movement repertoire takes its origin and impetus from the rhythm of his breathing. It is characterized by an

---

[45] Counter transference: "Behavior toward the other as if the self was the original object which affect was displaced," English, from Mosey, op. cit.

alternation of growing in free flow and shrinking in bound flow. Most mothers understand this pattern intuitively and react appropriately to it. However, there are some who interpret the shrinking sequence as rejection. Due to their own feelings of inadequacy, some mothers respond by rejecting their own infants. It is very easy to perceive the spiraling effect this may have on the primary object relationship. The mother, through her movements, deprives her child of experiencing the pleasure of his body in close physical contact with his parent (Lowen).

On the other hand, if the mother is over-possessive and smothering, the movement patterns of her infant may also be adversely affected, resulting in development of maladaptive behavior in later life. This mother may respond to the shrinking movement of the neonate by continually bulging her body. If, for example, the infant shrinks momentarily from the breast in order to swallow a large amount of milk and the mother responds by bulging her breast and pushing the nipple back into his mouth, the child will choke (Kestenberg). This domineering mother denies the baby his right to sense the power and pleasure of being a separate entity. She sees the infant as an object for her own personal pleasure (Lowen).

Dyadic Interaction Levels of Organization[46]

1. Egocentric

   The ability to perceive the mother figure when the mother figure is in the process of gratifying the needs of the self. At this level infantile needs are satisfied with minimal demands placed on the individual. (This then, is the anaclytic relationship).

2. Object-dependent

   The ability to trust and be dependent upon the mother figure. The individual's infantile needs are fulfilled. Human interaction is encouraged but broad limits are set for acceptable behavior.

3. Object-ambivalent

   The ability to trust and be dependent upon an authority figure. The individual's infantile needs are fulfilled but there is also some need frustration and a demand for socially acceptable behavior.

4. Semi-autonomous

   The ability to explore and interact in the environment in a relatively autonomous manner though remaining primarily dependent on the parental figures for satisfaction of socio-

[46] Concepts abstracted from Mosey.

emotional needs. The individual is required to interact with others in a protective environment while the dyadic partner continues to fulfill many of the individual's needs. [47]

5. Chumship

The ability to enter into a group relationship in which the other is experienced as important to the self and the needs of the other are felt as equal to the needs of the self. The dyadic partner encourages intimate interaction between dyads or triads of individuals but is not immediately involved in the interaction.

6. Autonomous

The ability to enter into a mutually need-satisfying relationship characterized by a firm commitment to the other which is maintained regardless of normal demands for sacrifice on the part of the self. The individual interacts in an unprotective environment and receives minimal need gratification from former dyadic partner.

Related Maladaptive Behavior with Suggested Methods and Techniques for Dance-Movement Therapy

1. Egocentric

Maladaptive Behavior: Difficulty in adaptively allowing the body to merge with the dyadic figure when that person is appropriately satisfying the individual's basic needs. For example, this may occur if the person is unable to form a trust relationship with anyone. Autistic children characteristically are unable to relate to any human and often treat people as non-human objects.

Dance-Movement Therapy Techniques:

1. Movement activities involving the therapist merging with the rhythms and flow of the individual. This entails an adjustment on the part of the therapist to the flow and rhythmic fluctuations of the individual in a manner which will allow them to develop.

   The therapist essentially duplicates the movements of the client. This says to the person that she is not placing any demands on him and wants only to be with him where he is. (All categories)

---

[47] During the oedipal phase roughly during 4-5 years of age, the triadic relationship of mother, father, and child comes into dominance; however, this facet of development will not be discussed due to the fact that there is usually only one movement therapist working with the client at a time.

2. Oral incorporative movements.[48] For example, the therapist holds the individual in a position similar to that utilized for the feeding of an infant. The therapist may then begin gradually to adapt the individual's tension flow rhythms to those of the normal sucking sequence. The therapist may also take the arms of the individual and move them in a gentle pumping fashion duplicating the neonatal associative global response to sucking. (All categories)

3. Movement activities involving the use of sounds. Although techniques may be done totally without the use of verbalization, a soothing humming or phonetic response which duplicates the rhythm being developed may also aid in reinforcing the appropriate organization of this level. (All categories)

Related elements: One-to-one group, use of flow of breath, enactive level of cognition, use of tension flow and symmetrical shape flow, and investment of positive affect,[49] oral libidinal, birth ritual process.

2. Object-dependent

A. Maladaptive Behavior: Difficulty in adaptively perceiving a differentiation between the self and the need-gratifying object; such as, the child continually merging with the therapist, falling almost limply into her arms, not sensing where the therapist ends and he begins. He may be unable to initiate a movement pattern without the physical aid of the dyadic partner.

Dance-Movement Therapy Techniques:

Movement activities which assist the individual in perceiving the differentiation by self and therapist. For example, the therapist makes use of various forms of stimulation, such as touching (tactile), use of mirror (visual) temperature (icing), etc. (all categories, except neurotic).

B. Maladaptive Behavior: Difficulty in adaptively cessating movement patterns which are representational of those produced in a mother-child dyad; e.g., a predominance of rocking and sucking patterns.

---

[48] See Flow Rhythms Levels of Organization; section on Oral Rhythms.
[49] See Body Image Levels of Organization; Primary Level.

81

Dance-Movement Therapy Techniques:

Use of patterns of an oral aggressive nature. [50] Patterns such as tapping various parts of the body, or tapping the floor or therapist. Seizing and letting go of objects and imagery which makes use of blowing out of air; e.g., being the wind or a balloon (children, psychotic).

Related elements: Body Image: differentiation of the body from the environment, one-to-one group, enactive level of cognition, oral aggressive rhythms, weaning ritual process.

3. Object-ambivalent

Maladaptive Behavior: Inappropriate negative response to authority figures. For example, an individual who is always refusing to do what a boss suggests at work; someone who is always being fired because of arguments with his superior.

Dance-Movement Therapy Techniques:

1. Movement situations which allow the client an opportunity to express negative feelings toward an authority in an imaginary movement drama which allows the client to be the victor. For example, the client may wish to recall a conflict situation between the father and himself; with a foam pillow acting as the father the individual could slash and kick it releasing his anger and gaining insight into his distortion of authority relationships (adult, neurotic).

2. Movement activities which facilitate the particular pattern for this level of organization. For example, movement activities involving the decrease of repetition of rhythms by anticipating patterns of lower frequency and promoting a delay in their repetition. [51] (All categories)

Related elements: One-to-one, parallel group, enactive or iconic levels of cognition, flow rhythms: anal sadistic.

4. Semi-autonomous

A. Maladaptive Behavior: Difficulty in adaptively moving into a group situation; someone, who for example, shies away from any kind of group experience.

---

[50] See Flow Rhythms Levels of Organization: Oral Aggressive section.

[51] This decrease in the repetition of rhythms is needed for the promotion of purposeful actions (Kestenberg). See Flow Rhythms: Anal Sadistic Phase for more specific examples.

Dance-Movement Therapy Techniques:

Dance activities which involve the person in a small parallel group. This group would remain leader directed. At times the therapist would respond on a one-to-one level with each of the members, similar to a class situation. (All categories)

Related elements:

Use of:

Spatial pre-efforts and horizontal directional shape;

Gravitational pre-efforts and vertical directional shape;

Temporal pre-efforts and sagittal directional shape.

Enactive or iconic level of cognition.

5. Chumship

Maladaptive Behavior: Difficulty in adaptively interacting with group members.

Dance-Movement Therapy Techniques:

1. Dance activities with female group and other more stereotypically masculine movement sequences with a male group; such as, a drama-movement group. (All categories)

2. Movement activities involving interaction between dyads or small subgroups of individuals which are not immediately involved with the therapist. Such as, suggest for them to explore in two's the use of a particular effort showing them the pattern, then after a while have two dyads join together, etc., etc. (All categories)

Related elements:

Use of:

Spatial efforts and horizontal shaping;

Weight efforts and vertical shaping;

Temporal efforts and sagittal shaping.

Iconic level of cognition, task group.

6. Autonomous

Maladaptive Behavior: Difficulty in adaptively tolerating the dependency of another on the self. For example, the inability to adjust the individual's own movement patterns to those of another in a nurturing, need-satisfying relationship.

Dance-Movement Therapy Techniques:

Movement activities involving the individual in a need-satisfying role with another or other individuals—usually members of an established group.

For example, suggest to the group to pair off e.g., "Pair off with whoever's eyes you meet." Then involve them in a reciprocal pleasure giving activity such as the touching or light slapping-tapping of the partner. [52] (All categories where appropriate)

Related elements: Egocentric cooperative group, iconic and abstract level of cognition. Use of all possible effort-shape combinations.

PRIMARY GROUP LEVELS OF ORGANIZATION

Certainly, one of the most basic adaptive behavior needed in our society is the ability to function adequately in a variety of primary groups. The presence of an aggregate of individuals scheduled for Movement Therapy affords the therapist the opportunity to observe, evaluate and teach them the component related material to obtain these levels of organization. However, most groups led by dance therapists seem to remain on a basic one-to-one or parallel level of functioning.

There are often several valid reasons for group Movement Therapy being maintained at this most basic level. For example, the individuals may not be capable of functioning on a higher, more organized level; the group may not be a stable unit—members may be constantly absent or the turnover too great; the members may lack investment and involvement; the purpose, goals or contract of the group may not be clear to its participants producing a sense of ambiguity.

There are numerous other factors as well; however, all of the above as well as many of those not mentioned may be remedied and rendered invalid if the therapist commits himself to alleviating them. And if one is committed to therapy and to working with his clients, he is committed to working through these problems as well.

Group Levels of Organization[53]

1. One-to-one

As mentioned before, the one-to-one level of group functioning is the most basic. It requires the interaction of the

---

[52] Be very sure the activity suggested is pleasure receiving for both members.

[53] Concepts abstracted from Mosey.

individual with the other person (usually the therapist) either alone or in the presence of others. No demands are placed on the individual to interact in any way with the other members.

2. Parallel Group

The parallel level also mentioned requires that the individual now be able to attend to his own needs in the presence of others.

3. Task Group

This level requires that the individual now incorporate the ability to participate in short-term tasks with others with no demands made on him to continue the relationship outside of the designated task period. Although the leader still continues to meet the emotional needs of each member, he is now responsible for encouraging interaction among the individual members.

4. Egocentric and Group Cooperative

This level involves the ability to interact in a long-term task which entails not only the awareness of self interest but also the ability to satisfy defined needs of others in the group. The group is generally encouraged to make independent decisions in choosing tasks or immediate goals; however, general suggestions can be made initially when the fear of failure may be prevalent. The therapist's role is still that of support and general satisfaction of the socio-emotional needs of the members; however, with the advent of the gratification of an individual's needs by others in the group, he may evolve himself into the role of a catalyst or advisor.

Related Maladaptive Behavior with Suggested Methods and Techniques for Dance-Movement Therapy

1. One-to-one Group

Maladaptive Behavior: Inability to adaptively engage in Dance-Movement Therapy in the presence of others.

Dance-Movement Therapy Techniques:

1. Allow the individual to observe the dance therapy session. If he is unwilling to move, suggest to him to select a record or to duplicate some of the beats or patterns that the group is doing while he is sitting. Let him know even though he isn't up dancing with the rest, that he is still very much part of the group. Acknowl-

edge his presence during the session as well as at the end. (All categories)

2. Movement activities involving the manipulation of the individual by the therapist to promote body awareness and body image organization. For example, the therapist may stimulate the individual kinesthetically by moving his extremities through various shapes. (All categories)

Related elements: Object dependent or supportive relationship with therapist, enactive or iconic level of cognition.

2. Parallel Group

Maladaptive Behavior: Difficulty in adaptively sharing the movement session with others; a person for example, who cannot attend to his own needs in the presence of others.

Dance-Movement Therapy Techniques:

1. Movement activities involving the meeting of the socio-emotional needs of each member. The therapist "picks up" the movement patterns of each individual and adapts them. For example, if the therapist observes a patient's movements becoming more aggressive, he may develop the sequence into a more strong, direct, quick pattern. (All categories)

2. Movement activities which involve each member attending to his own needs in the presence of others. This can be at an extremely basic level; such as, a suggestion for everyone to walk about the room at their own pace and in their own way. (All categories)

Related elements: Semi-autonomous or supportive relationship with therapist; enactive or iconic level of cognition.

3. Task Group

Maladaptive Behavior: Difficulty in adaptively involving himself in short term tasks. This could be an individual who continuously moves into the center of the circle during a Dance Therapy session dancing in an exhibitionistic manner, or one who is always in competition with others for the leadership role.

Dance-Movement Therapy Techniques:

1. Dance sessions which afford the individual(s) an opportunity to be the leader such as when the leadership is passed around the group (when one member is finished

87

Figure III-10. Group Cooperative: Psycho-motor Technique.

he passes it to a person near him and all must follow the next member's movements). (All categories)

2. Movement activities involving short-term tasks. For example, if the group is large divide it into subgroups of 4—suggest a task; e.g., all be part of something that moves, have them show this for the rest of the members to guess (all categories; however not applicable for most psychotics).

Related elements: Supportive relationship with therapist; i.e., semi-autonomous, encouragement of chumship, enactive and/or iconic, levels of cognition.

4. Egocentric and Group Cooperative

Maladaptive Behavior: Difficulty in adaptively taking on a variety of membership roles. This could be someone who could follow well but who had difficulty assuming a leadership capacity.

Dance-Movement Therapy Techniques:

1. Movement activities involving the ability of the individual to take on various roles and/or accommodate to the needs of other members. For example, each member may be given an opportunity to stage some situation that has occurred; the other members of the group are used as substitutes for the actual individuals or objects involved. The individual is then allowed to propose an alternate ending to the usually emotionally charged encounter. The other members chosen to participate must be ready to act as negative or ideal figures depending on the needs of the enactor. For example, he may wish him to cower from an imaginary inflicted punch or to respond with a friendly embrace. Through this often symbolic process of resolution, the individuals will learn that they are capable of satisfying their own needs and the needs of others (Pesso) (adult, neurotics). (See Figures III, #10, on the previous page.)

2. Movement activities designed for occupational search. For example, the session may be devoted to the explaining, through active body involvement of the members, the necessary movement repertoire for a desired job (adults, neurotics, patient's leaving hospital).

The group membership should be consistent with an ideal range of 5-8 members.

Related elements: Autonomous dyadic relationship, iconic and/or abstract levels of cognition.

DRIVE-OBJECT LEVELS OF ORGANIZATION[54]

In order to satisfy primary and secondary needs,[55] an individual must be able to assemble and govern the necessary energy to acquire the appropriate need-satisfying objects. This energy or drive, as it is often called, is generally considered to be in two forms: libidinal drive, which is directed toward need-fulfilling objects; and aggressive drive, which is directed toward any object which "gets in the way" of acquiring need satisfaction.

Since much need gratification involves the channeling of the psychic energy through the motor apparatus, Movement Therapy directed toward the organization of the needed adapted components can be of great assistance to a struggling individual. With each motor sequence comes a change in the inner psychic situation which serves either to bring him closer or farther away from appropriate direction of psychic energy. It is up to the therapist to be aware of the amount of energy being expended by the client and to know whether or not the quantum allotted is appropriate for the given task. Psychic energy may exist in every human being; however, because of its employment in the service of an over-used defense mechanism[56] such as repression or withdrawal, the individual may appear to be lifeless. Assuming that he is energyless serves only to perpetuate maladaptive behavior and further impede the free flow of energy which could be appropriately cathected and directed toward either a libidinal or aggressive object.[57]

This is one area with which dance therapists are often involved; for this reason, if for no other, it is important to have a clear picture about the necessary components needed in the acquisition of the various levels. All too often a therapist may struggle to bring about a catharsis of aggressive drive without awareness of the individual's need for libidinal investment.

[54] Adapted from Mosey.

[55] Primary needs: nourishment, shelter, sexual satisfaction, elimination, self-esteem, riciprocal love relationship(s) (Maslow); secondary needs grow out of primary needs, such as financial security or power.

[56] Defense mechanisms "are learned patterns of behavior and mental operations which help the individual to deal with conflicts between needs, drives, and cultural norms" (Mosey). They are, in other words, ego mediators between the libido (needs, drives) and the superego (rules, norms, taboos, etc.). It should also be stressed here that defense mechanisms, when utilized properly, are desired additions to a functioning ego. For example, without the mechanism of sublimation, the role of Dance Therapy would certainly be impeded.

[57] A clear example of this phenomena is the person who never seems to respond in an anger provoking situation. His body is held in a rigid bound state. It is as if he was literally using the energy in an inner battle: agonists contracted wanting to strike out and antagonists contracted keeping him from doing so due to possible fear, guilt, or a double bind situation.

Drive Object Levels of Organization

1. Investment of Libidinal Drive in Self

   This involves the ability to place libidinal energy in the self. It is characteristic of secondary narcissism of the infant in which he perceives himself as the need gratifying object. He feels himself to be omnipotent and sees the mother figure as an extension of himself.

2. Investment of Libidinal Drive in External Objects

   This involves the ability to place libidinal psychic energy in objects other than the self. The drive is first directed toward the primary object, the nurturing mother figure, and then to other objects, human as well as non-human.

3. Investment of Aggressive Drive in External Objects

   This level entails the capacity to place aggressive energy in objects other than the self. The primary object is often the one to be experimented upon, especially if her attentions are directed elsewhere for a period of time. In order for this behavior to be properly integrated, the individual's use of the drive must prove to be successful to some extent. It must also be controlled so that the individual is aware of what may be destroyed or physically affected and what should not be.

Related Maladaptive Behavior with Suggested Methods and Techniques for Dance Movement Therapy

1. Investment of Libidinal Drive in Self

   A. Maladaptive Behavior: Inappropriate inhibition of libidinal rhythms (usually established in infancy, such as early inhibition of autoerotic sucking).

   Dance-Movement Therapy Techniques:

   Movement activities involving the use of libidinal rhythms. Such as holding oneself and rocking to a lullaby. (All categories)

   B. Maladaptive Behavior: Non-verbal cues which suggest an inappropriate lack of care of self; for example, unkempt clothing and hair, or poor hygenic care. These characteristics often go along with feelings of worthlessness and a flaccid limp or bound body attitude; such that there is a loss of elasticity.

Dance-Movement Therapy Techniques:

1. Activities involving tactile stimulation reinforced by positive verbalizations concerning the body. As in face-telling when the therapist touches each portion of a person's face and describes it in detail in a gentle supportive tone, e.g., "And near where your forehead ends and your eyes begin are dark brown eyebrows. They are shiny and very soft to touch. They fall in a flowing arch which follows the line of your eyes" (all categories except tactilely defensive individuals). (See Figure III, #11, below.)

Figure III-11. Face Telling.

2. Movement activities involving the use of indulging pre-efforts:

<u>Pre-efforts</u>

flexibility

gentleness

hesitation

(All categories)

Related elements: Egocentric relationship with therapist; corresponding directional shape and shaping; flow of breath; body-image: investment of positive affect, enactive cognition, tactile perception.

2. Investment of Libidinal Drive in External Objects

   Maladaptive Behavior: Difficulty in adaptively using indulging efforts and the corresponding shaping when with people.
   This then would be someone who might have a great deal
   of difficulty relating to others in a positive manner. He
   might relate only on an aggressive level or be unable to
   relate at all.

   Dance-Movement Therapy Techniques:

   Movement activities which utilize indulging efforts and
   corresponding shaping in various combinations in a
   dyadic and group experience.

Effort	Shaping
indirect	spreading
light	rising
sustained	advancing

   The therapist may want to suggest to the group to move
   toward the center of the circle using the above combination (if age appropriate) which might be followed by
   each member saying "Hello" to his fellow members
   when all had reached the center. (All categories)

   Or the therapist may suggest that the group form dyads
   and have a non-verbal conversation using the above
   combinations. Use of a scarf or towel which both may
   hold is often of help as well as music with a soft flowing
   quality. (All categories)

   Related elements: Object-dependent relationship with
   therapist; one-to-one or parallel group.

3. Investment of Aggressive Drive in External Objects

   A. Maladaptive Behavior: A body attitude of inappropriate
   bound flow particularly in the jaw, shoulders, chest,
   and/or legs along with insistence that the individual in
   question never gets angry. These people might have a
   great deal of fear about "letting go" with aggressive
   behavior. Quite often if there is no sublimated outlet
   for the aggressive energy, they actually feel that if they
   did finally "let go," they would not be able to control
   themselves and might destroy the environment around
   them.

   Dance-Movement Therapy Techniques:

   Movement activities involving gradual release of welled
   up aggressive energy. For example, the therapist might

start on a gestural level stressing the fighting efforts and corresponding shaping that the person feels most comfortable. And gradually as the individual trusts more his control mechanisms; the therapist can evolve him into more of a gestural-posture merging of the patterns. It is relevant to note here that if the individual does lose control and there seems to be a possibility of his hurting himself or others, the therapist may assist the person by:

1. redirecting the strong-quick-direct pattern such as suggesting to him to "stamp your feet" or "hit the pillow" or

2. evolving the individual into the utilization of more indulging qualities such as changing the attitude toward space from directness to indirectness producing a slash; or from strength to lightness producing a dab; or from quickness to sustainment producing a press; or

3. the evolving of a postural pattern into a gestural one. (All categories)

B. Maladaptive Behavior: Difficulty in adaptively moving utilizing the fighting pre-efforts and corresponding directions and the fighting efforts with corresponding shaping. This might be characteristic of someone who is described as depressed. When and if they do utilize fighting efforts, they may be always on a gestural level; or they may even turn their anger in on themselves (retro-flexed rage) and take on self-mutilating behavior such as biting their nails or head banging.

Dance-Movement Therapy Techniques:

1. Use of the fighting pre-efforts, efforts and the corresponding shape and shaping:

Pre-effort	Directional Shape
channelled	side across body
vehemence	downwards
suddenness	backwards

Effort	Shaping
direct	enclosing
strong	sinking
quick	retreating

94

For example, gross movements such as kicking, pushing, slashing, punching, seizing, chopping, stamping, or hitting an imaginary object. (All categories)

2. Traveling movements involving getting imaginary objects out of the pathway.

   For example, place pillows on the floor and have the individual kick them out of his path. He may wish to use verbalizations such as, "Get out of my way!" (All categories)

3. Circle movement activities involving release of directed aggressive energy. For example, have each member place his hands on the shoulders of the persons next to him. The circle should then gradually move from side to side with each person pushing off the shoulder of the person he is leaning toward. After momentum is built up, take the movement into the whole body (all categories except individual). (See Figure III, #12, below.)

Figure III-12. Shoulder Push-Pull.

Or, one individual is placed in the center of the circle; the other members close in tight. The individual is asked to get out of the circle (group, adult, children, neurotic).

Related elements: Object-ambivalent, semi-autonomous, or autonomous relationship with therapist. The therapist should know when to control uncontrolled behavior and when to allow aggressive release of energy. By protecting an individual from diffuse aggressive outbursts, the person will be relieved of the guilt which would proceed from the experience (Dr. Rosen). Parallel, task or egocentric cooperative group.

BODY-IMAGE LEVELS OF ORGANIZATION

A healthy body image is one of the most important factors in the development of a functioning individual. It is contingent on many elements; among them, libidinal investment in the body, awareness of the body and its functions, effective control of primary process material, and other opinions of the self including cultural norms concerning physical attractiveness.

So much of the organization of this area occurs through movement, whether it be of a purely functional or emotional basis. Paul Schilder, who conceptualized the term body-image, writes, "Motion influences the body-image and leads the person from a change in the body-image to a change in the psychic attitude."[58]

The importance of Dance-Movement Therapy is obvious. However, like many areas of adaptive development, there exists a sequential progression of levels which must be fully organized if the person is to have an adequate body-image. Therefore, improvement in this area cannot always be assumed just because the person attends Dance Therapy. Without sensitive awareness of the level of adaptive functioning of an individual, movement may even prove to exacerbate the existing problems. For example, on certain occasions body motion may be a destructive element in the formulation of a body-image. Movement can become a terrifying occurrence if the individual perceives his body as dissolving with every step he takes. Keeping his body silent for a period of time might be the only securing factor, particularly when he is placed in an environment to which he is unaccustomed. [59]

Familiarity in the observation of the movement patterns through which the individual reveals his body-image is a vital and needed skill. The changes in shaping which are exhibited can tell the therapist where his focus should be in order to evolve his client to a higher, more appropriate level of functioning.

---

[58] Paul Schilder, The Image and Appearance of the Human Body (New York: John Wiley and Sons, Inc., 1964), p. 208.

[59] Ibid., p. 301.

Body Image Levels of Organization

1. Investment of Positive Affect in Body

   This level involves the capacity to perceive the body as a positive object. It entails libidinal investment in the physical properties of the self. The integration of this level is contingent upon the non-verbal communication of the primary object concerning the acceptability of the individual's body and bodily functionings, i. e., secondary narcissism.

2. Differentiation of the Body from the Environment

   This involves the capacity to perceive the difference between what is physically part of the self and what is the "other." Initially it entails the departure from the narcissistic omnipotent world of an infant with the disassociation of the primary object, the mother figure. This is followed by further disassociation from the remainder of the environment.

3. Recognition of Body Parts and Their Interrelationship

   This level involves the functioning knowledge of the body, its parts, and how they relate to one another. The acquisition of this ability thus entails the ability to differentiate various parts of the body in terms of their placement and function. Awareness of as well as the differentiation between that part of the body which is internal and that which is external is also considered part of this level.

4. Movement of the Body Through Space

   This level entails the ability to adequately move the body through space toward a desired goal. This involves adequate motor planning as well as functioning knowledge of distance, weight, space, and time. The organization of this level is contingent upon the integration of both sides of the body freeing the individual to involve himself in activities which entail movements at and across the midline. At this atage a feeling of being the master of one's being becomes apparent.

5. Sexual Identity

   This level involves the capacity of the individual to perceive his or her sexuality. This entails not only acknowledgement and libidinization of the appropriate gender but, eventually, identification with a person of the same sex as well as the capacity for heterosexual involvement.

1. Investment of Positive Affect

A. Maladaptive Behavior: Minimal or lack of adaptive libidinal investment in one's body. For example, there
are many who perceive themselves as bad, dirty, worthless. They are continuously depressed with a slumped
and/or bound body—a characteristic signal for the therapist. This means that underlying the sadness is a deep
retro-flexed rage or anger turned inward. This anger
might only demonstrate itself via psycho-somatic complaints such as tension, ulcers, colitis, etc., but is
none-the-less very much present within the organism.

Dance-Movement Therapy Techniques:

1. Movement activities involving adaptive tension and shape
flow with G-P merging. [60] Such as discussed in the
Flow of Breath.

2. Movement activities designed to map out, shape, clarify, and work through dead spots or areas of somatic
complaints which may be thought to hold cathectic psychic energy. For example, if the client blocks her
breathing in the gut area or complains of being sick to
her stomach all the time or has continuous acid attacks,
the therapist might ask the client to "look inside" her
stomach and describe the feeling and what she sees.
The response could be; "It's very dark, I can't see
anything" or "It's like a whirlpool in there. Everything
is churning around." The therapist might then ask if
she could pretend that this darkness could talk what
would it say. The conversation could be helped to start
by saying e.g., "I am darkness in Sally's (client)
stomach; I am here because . . ." Sally might
answer, "because I don't want Sally to know what's
behind my darkness." A conversation might then develop which would lead to a movement exercise e.g.,
growing into the darkness through to the other side or
doing battle with the somatic defense (adults, neurotic,
individual) (Gestalt).

B. Maladaptive Behavior: Difficulty in adaptively formulating interpersonal relationships. The rational for
this person's difficulty is the lack of an adequate pri-

---

[60] G-P: Gesture-Posture.

mary object relationship with the mother which showed itself in part by the mother responding to her child as if her body were something to be touched only in a functional manner. This is the mother who may later become upset with the child's masturbatory inclinations. This is the mother who usually feels negatively about her own body. Thus the client may have difficulty relating to the therapist.

Dance-Movement Therapy Techniques:

1. Movement activities which incorporate the therapist touching the person's body. For example; if the client has much bound tension in his body, the therapist might have him sit in a chair or lie on a mat. She might then suggest to relax and go limp. To test this relaxation out the therapist gently picks up body parts such as the arms and passively rocks them at the shoulder joint to detect how loose and "unbound" they are. The head is also held and rolled in the socket. The therapist quietly speaks to the client telling him if the transitions are smooth or if there is a block. Reassuring the person that the therapist can hold onto the body parts without his aid is sometimes important as well (adults, neurotic, psychotic, individual). (See Figure III, #13, below.)

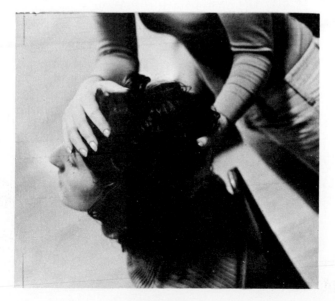

Figure III-13.

99

2. Movement activities involving gathering, grasping, and other incorporative motions. This is very workable in groups in which the acceptability of having a right to reach and take is reinforced by the other members. (All categories)

Related elements: Use of oral rhythms; flow of breath; Drive-object: libidinal investment in self; use of tactile stimulation, holding and rocking; egocentric relationship with therapist; one-to-one or parallel group, weaning ritual process.

2. Differentiation of the Body from the Environment

A. Maladaptive Behavior: Body boundaries lack adaptive bound tension flow and shrinking in shape flow. This is a person who is unable to differentiate his body from his surroundings. He is continually merging with the environment.

Dance-Movement Therapy Techniques:

1. Movement activities which stress the use of bound tension flow and shrinking in shape flow. Such as, gradually tensing and relaxing of various body parts or suggestions to close up tight like a ball. (All categories) (See Figure III, #14, below.)

2. Tactile and or temperature stimulation of the body using various textures such as a towel or soft brush. (All categories)

Figure III-14. "Like a Ball."

100

3. Activities involving the individual physically exploring that which is part of his body and that which is the "other." For example, the therapist might sit or stand with a child in front of a mirror affording him further cues (child, individual, psychotic).

4. Movement activities involving verbal and physical assertion of what is the self and what is not. For example, going around a circle, one at a time, each turning to the person next to him yelling, "I am me! Who are you!" (Chace). (All categories)

B. Maladaptive Behavior: Fear that portions of the body are not attached but are floating. This is an individual who has really depersonalized; if asked to raise his arms he might refuse and if he is able to verbalize he might say that they would drift away if he did what the therapist asked.

Dance-Movement Therapy Activities:

Techniques which involve reinforcement that the body is a totality and will not float away.

a. Have the individual view himself in a mirror (visual) or lie on the floor (tactile) while moving the body part while the therapist gives proprioceptive stimulation of body part with continuous pushing of the part back into the joint; e.g., pushing arm back into shoulder joint (all categories appropriate for psychotics). (See Figure III, #15, p. 102.)

b. Pressure stimulation in which the therapist places his hands one in the front of the body and one behind. Both hands touch and leave the part simultaneously. (All categories)

Related elements: Oral aggressive rhythms, regulation of tension flow and shape flow, perceptual stimulation, object-dependent relationship with therapist, one-to-one or parallel group.

3. Recognition of Body Parts and Their Interrelationship

A. Maladaptive Behavior: Cannot recognize or name body parts and/or organize their relationship.

Dance-Movement Therapy Techniques:

1. Movement activities involving the use of specific body parts—use of games similar to "Simon says." (children, psychotic, group, individual, retarded)

101

Figure III-15. Kinesthetic Stimulation.

2. Movement activities in which the therapist inquires about the functions of body parts; for example, "Show me what a hand can do," etc. (All categories)

3. Activities involving the therapist taking a person passively through a desired pattern followed by his repeating the pattern. (All categories)

4. Dance activities involving the use of a bar, such as with leg range of motion swings. (All categories)

5. Discussion and experiential use of various body parts nomenclature graded on complexity:

body	front	bottom	hand	waist
skin	back	head	shoulder	leg
hair	side	neck	chest	foot
teeth	top	arms	stomach	hip, etc.

so that the individual may be able to touch, sight, name, experience kinesthetically, and explore the general function. (All categories)

6. Discussion of physical differences in a group. Such as, size of feet, color of eyes, etc. (All categories)

7. Movement activities involving the use of rhythm instruments, the making of rhythm sounds by the body, and/or music; such as:

   a. clapping, beat by tongue (All categories)

   b. having them establish their own rhythm such as to their name, and see if they can all duplicate each other's (retarded, children, psychotic).

   c. hold hands, one person sends a beat, the others pass it around the circle. (All categories)

   d. variation exploration: quick-slow or loud or soft. (All categories)

   e. acting out action songs (children, groups).

B. Maladaptive Behavior: Unawareness of and/or inability to differentiate between that which is the internal body and that which is external body. This could be someone who can only understand what he sees and is frightened of and/or does not understand what he cannot see.

Dance-Movement Therapy Techniques:

1. Discussion of relationship and palpation of parts of the body which are internal and parts external such as:

skin	bone
hair	muscle
nails	viscera: stomach, etc.
teeth	fascia: fat, etc.

(All categories)

2. Activities involving the awareness of the internal body image. For example, ask the person to lie down and relax. Then suggest to him to become aware of his breathing. Ask him then to follow the passage of air throughout his body. The therapist may mention the parts of the body in sequential fashion. The same method may be used in the digestion of an imaginary morsel of food (Yoga). (All categories)

C. Maladaptive Behavior: Perceptions and distortions of the body-image; such as, body or body parts felt to be larger or smaller, fatter or thinner, more rigid or wavy, more or less (may use self-portrait as indicator).

Dance-Movement Therapy Techniques:

1. Activities involving the creating and use of a self portrait; such as:

   a. Have the person draw or sculpt a self-figure. Stimulus: "Draw yourself" or "make yourself with this clay." Then have him look at himself in the mirror seeing and discussing what is similar and what is dissimilar. (All categories)

   b. The therapist draws an outline of the person while he is lying on or standing next to a large full-length piece of paper (roll of brown wrapping paper is useful here). The client then draws in the rest. (All categories especially children)

2. Autoscopy: Ask the individual to close his eyes and imagine himself standing or sitting in front of him. Ask him to describe what he sees (Schilder). Then have him look at himself and play back for him if possible, his description. Discuss the relationship (adults, individuals, neurotics).

Related elements: Asymmetrical shape flow; pre-efforts and directional shape; perceptual stimulation; one-to-one or parallel group, object-ambivalent relationship with therapist.

4. Movement of the Body Through Space

A. Maladaptive Behavior: Uncoordinated adaptive movement through space on a gestural and/or postural level. This could be someone who cannot effectively combine body parts and the relationship of the dynamics and shape of movement effectively to get to a desired goal in space or to do a task.

Dance-Movement Therapy Techniques:

Movement activities involving the use of effort-shape affinities and combinations. The therapist observes at which level of effort-shape organization the individual is. He also notes which qualities the individual prefers to use and develops activities around those. The therapist must always be aware of the difference between facilitating the organization of a particular attribute or quality and attempting to superimpose a novel repertoire which is not ego syntonic (refer to effort, shape, and posture-gesture for further specifics). (All categories)

B. Maladaptive Behavior: Difficulty in adaptive motor planning; for example, someone who has difficulty moving from one place to another without continuously bumping into and/or tripping over objects.

Dance-Movement Therapy Techniques:

1. Activities involving motor planning. For example, the therapist may set up a real or hypothetical obstacle course which the person must go through. They can go through forward, backward, eyes closed, etc. (See Figure III, #16, p. 106.) (All categories)

2. Experience in various locomotor activities; such as hopping, walking, skipping, galloping, marching, etc. (there are specific records available for these activities). (All categories)

3. Group activities which involve the following of various directions such as, "move to the center of the circle." "Form a line" or "move while holding your feet." These suggestions may be graded in complexity such as "sit with your back against the wall and one foot on the floor." (All categories)

4. Use of related games such as musical chairs or charades. (All categories)

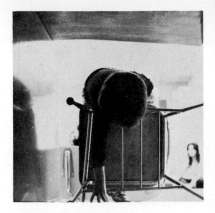

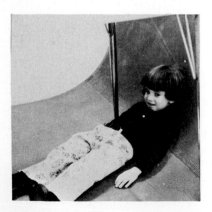

Figure III-16. Motor Planning: Obstacle Course.

106

C. Maladaptive Behavior: Laterality dominance and/or inability to adaptively move reciprocally. This is seen when an individual is unable to cross the midline of his body.

Dance-Movement Therapy Techniques:

Activities involving reciprocal movement as well as movement which crosses the midline of the body. For example:

a. Reciprocal swinging of arms or "bicycling" with legs when on back. (All categories)

b. Dyadic shoulder push pull: both individuals have their hands on each other's shoulder, both push with right arm then left. This same pattern can be done lying down feet to feet. (All categories)

c. Placing 2 color tile blocks or 2 color shoe prints on the floor, e.g., red for right leg blue for left. Instruct the person to follow the path stepping only on the appropriate blocks (which involve the crossing of the right over the left and the left over the right at various times). (All categories)

d. "Simon says touch your elbows" (children).

Related elements: Effort-shape combinations, one-to-one, parallel, or task group; semi-autonomous relationship with therapist.

5. Sexual Identity

A. Maladaptive Behavior: Lack of appropriate presence or difficulty with adaptive sex-specific inner-genital and phallic rhythms. This could be an individual who, for various reasons, might have either denied his or her sexuality, identified with a person of the opposite sex, or had minimal or no sexual identification with a a same-sex model (asexual).

Dance-Movement Therapy Techniques:

Movement activities which emphasize culturally designated sex specific movement patterns. It should be noted here that both inner-genital and phallic rhythms as well as all efforts and shapes are needed by both sexes for a fully adaptive behavioral repertoire. However, their segregated use may assist in the individual's expression of feminity or masculinity.

Feminine		Masculine
inner-genital rhythms		phallic rhythms
light		strong
slow	efforts	quick
indirect		direct
inclusive behavior		intrusive behavior
enclosing, surrounding		piercing, going
circles		through, leaps

(All categories)

Use of imagery and records which are symbolic of masculine or feminine nature. Such as, the bull or snake for a man and a butterfly or cat for a woman. (All categories)

B. Maladaptive Behavior: Maladaptive rigid posturing produced by a tense pelvic area. This person often has difficulty giving or receiving sexual gratification.

Dance-Movement Therapy Techniques:

Movement activities involving the release and movement of the pelvic area.

a. Positions which produce spontaneous movements of the pelvic area. Such as the position of hyperextension designed by Lowen. (See Figure III, #17, below.) The thighs begin to vibrate due to muscle fatigue producing

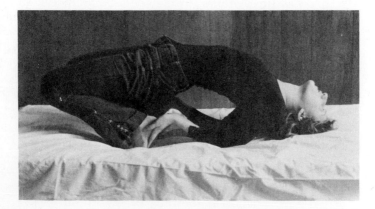

Figure III-17.

108

a free undulating up/down movement of the pelvis. [61] (adult, neurotic, individual)

b. Dancing which involves movement of the pelvic region; e.g., Latin, rock, or African dances. (All categories)

Related elements: Semi-autonomous or autonomous relationship with therapist; parallel task, or ego-centric cooperative group, puberty ritual process.

RITES OF PASSAGE LEVELS OF ORGANIZATION

One way of looking at and working with a therapeutic developmental process is the viewing of individual evolution as a working through of a series of crises or milestones which correspond with key phases in the life of a human being. Society has often facilitated the progression and integration of these milestones through the use of rituals or rites of passage. Turner's Ritual Process elaborately states how the ritual process helps people to exist and to find their way in the complexities of organized culture. Recurrent in the work of Erikson is a fascination with how rituals introduce and aid the fledgling into becoming a member of a society at large, then further guides that person through life and even into death. [62]

It is quite relevant that movement is used as an avenue for rituals within therapy since dance has traditionally been one of the most widely utilized media for rites of passage.

Role identification, replacement, and reversal, as well as basic catharsis—classic techniques in movement therapy—have all evolved from ancient ritual ceremonies. It is not surprising then that Jungian dance and psychomotor therapists have been making use of ritual for some time. [63] Whether conceptualized is an arch typal myth or a structure, [64] recapitulation of crucial periods involving symbolic rites of passage has often proven through the ages to be of therapeutic necessity.

At a time when western man has eliminated or so-sapped the meaning out of what developmental ceremonies remain, it behooves the dance movement therapist to recultivate the seeds of these processes which have been sown so many years ago.

---

[61] Lowen, op. cit., Betrayal of the Body pp. 244-245.

[62] Penny Bernstein and Lawrence Bernstein. "A Conceptualization of Group Dance-Movement Therapy as a Ritual Process" ADTA Monograph Volume III. 1974.

[63] Jungian Dance Therapy originated with Mary Whitehouse in California. Since then students, such as Janet Adler Boettiger, have utilized and expanded this method.

[64] Structure: Pesso-Psychomotor Therapy—a motoric recapitalation of past or fantasized events in which target figures are polarized permitting expression of what was not expressed in actuality.

RITES OF PASSAGE LEVELS OF ORGANIZATION

1. Birth Ritual Process

   Birth here is defined as the process through which an individual is born from a lesser to a higher, more fuller, level of life, awareness, and self-actualization.

2. Weaning Ritual Process

   The process through which an individual evolves from a state of dependence to that of autonomy from the primary or surrogate objects.

3. Puberty Ritual Process

   Initiation through precept and ritual from childhood into adult life, along with its corresponding sexual mores and societal demands and roles.

4. Marriage Ritual Process

   This entails a mutual commitment with another in a long-term need satisfying, intimate heterosexual relationship.

5. Retirement Ritual Process

   This process involves the gradual separation of an individual's active involvement within his society concomitant with a progressive feeling of ego integrity. [65] An evolving sense of man's relationship to the cosmos and eternity reaches a level of crystallization such that death is seen as just another rite of passage into another evolutionary phase of existence.

Related Maladaptive Behavior with Suggested Methods and Techniques for Dance-Movement Therapy

1. Birth Ritual Process

   A. Maladapture Behavior: Repressed primal fear from birth trauma characterized by fear cathected into pockets of body tension or numbed dead spots. (Blocked fear may also be represented by bulging eyes and an elevated shoulder girdle.)

   Dance-Movement Therapy Techniques:

   Movement activities involving the release of repressed fear via a recapitulation of the birth processes. A heated pool is an excellent milieu for this ritual. The

---

[65] Ego Integrity, Erikson, Childhood and Society, p. 268-269.

designated individual should be held for several minutes
in a fetal position by a mother surrogate. Eyes should
be closed and the ears submerged, thereby blocking
out any outside stimuli. The person is moved slowly
and gently through the water. Loss of consciousness
will occur as sense of space, weight, and time dissi-
pates. Other members of the group stand in two parallel lines facing each other extending from the "mother;"
they act as a contracting human birth canal. Utilizing
feminine sadistic rhythms throughout their bodies,
they begin to push the "fetus" down the birth canal. A
"doctor" stands facing the mother at the opposite end of
the line and receives the individual headfirst. Where-
upon the "doctor" assisted by the rest of the group
members propels the individual up out of the water in a
vertical position and facilitates his grasp of reality and
life by insuring that he lands upright, on his feet,
grounded in reality. (See Figure 111-18.)

Figure III-18.

The individual should be allowed and encouraged to release his fear through screaming with the expelled air,
which has been breathed into and released from areas
tensed from repressed fear. (Normal to neurotic
adults.)

B. Maladaptive Behavior: Final struggles and frustration
regarding the working through of a particular conflict.
No matter what the conflict, many individuals find it
difficult to evolve from maladaptive behavior to more

111

adapture functioning even though a particular Gestalt involving the integration of a prior conflict has been resolved. The process of re-aggregation[66] or bringing the Gestalt into subliminal awareness needs a movement activity to facilitate that evolution.

Dance-Movement Therapy Techniques:

1. Movement activities involving verbal cues to the individual to facilitate a re-birth process. Such as: "You are in a small dark cave which has no room for you to stand. The way out is through a narrow tunnel. Be there and in your own time and your own way move into the sunshine."[67] (Neurotic adults and children.)

2. Movement activities involving group facilitation of the re-birth processes. Such as having group members create a womb-like environment for the individual from which he can grow from a closed to an open position. Group members may take the shape of the outside "petals" surrounding a "blossoming" individual. (All categories)

Related elements: Breath flow, symmetrical shape flow.

2. Weaning Ritual Process

A. Maladaptive Behavior: Life seems to be too painful and basic trust seems to be unavailable to the individual who has never fully weaned himself. They cannot seem to initiate any dyadic movement experiences when involved in group dance improvisations. The person may continuously place himself in a passive role in relationship to others.

Dance-Movement Therapy Techniques:

Dyadic movement rites involving the nurturing and rocking of the individual. Some therapists suggest that the individual being held, be allowed to suck on the fleshy part of the mother surrogate's arm. By allowing this nuturing process to be reenacted it is hoped that the individual will integrate the needed elements for the weaning process to occur. The mother surrogate may facilitate this process by rocking her "child" and assuring him that he may have all the sweet milk he needs. [68] (All categories)

[66] Reaggregation: final stage of ritual process, see Turner, Ritual Process, p. 72.

[67] Quite often the individual will evolve into this rebirth process on their own as the natural resolution and completion of a previously conflicted area. The ritual is easily detected during verbal sharing at the end of the session.

[68] Albert Pesso, Experience in Action.

112

B. Maladaptive Behavior: Inability to "take a stand" in relation to authority figures characterized by repressed hostility toward one or more parents. The individual is often fixated at an anal ambivalent phase exhibiting excessive use of the anal libidinal rhythm in pure and mixed form.

Dance-Movement Therapy Techniques:

1. Movement activities involving an autonomy rite of passage such as one of the support structures suggested by Pesso. [69] In order for the individual to feel comfortable about expressing repressed anger toward parental figures, each parent is split in two; group members become bad parents while others become his good parents supporting him in his cathartic expression of anger. Support may be both physical as well as verbal. The good parents may even initially help him emote by evolving the individual into strong, quick, direct patterns through synchronous, evolutionary movement. (Chace) The negative accomodators or "bad parents" may encourage the enactors angry release by saying that they are model parents or by denying every accusation (psychodrama). If they prove to be too strong adversaries, they can be instructed to cringe and whimper at even the mere suggestion of strength exhibited by the individual. The ritual may be completed by the enactor destroying the bad parents with the reinforcement and love from the good parents. (Adult neurotics)

2. Movement activity involving the ritual making and subsequent destruction of a life-size "mother." Adults and children. (When used with children, the figure may not necessarily be identified.)

3. Movement-drama activities in which the individual becomes the parent or symbolic figure of power. Quite often children will become monsters or wild animals capable of devouring and thereby incorporating the powerful therapists or any other authority figures (children).

   Related elements: Oral libidinal, anal sadistic flow rhythms, investment of positive affect, egocentric and object ambivalent relationship.

3. Puberty Ritual Process:

A. Maladaptive Behavior: Role confusion with a lack of a sense of identification within the transition from child-

[69] Ibid.

113

hood to adulthood may show itself behaviorally in imma-
ture child-like movements, excessive amounts of tension flow with difficulty in moving utilizing full-effort
actions. Clothing or self-drawing may be asexual and/
or infantile.

Dance-Movement Therapy Techniques:

1. Movement drama activities involving the trying on of
   numerous identities through the role playing of a variety of adult figures which may be ego ideals or heroes
   of the individuals. Other group members may be asked
   to respond in previously designated manners to the particular individual. (Adolescent)

2. Movement activities involving reenactment of myths or
   culturally appropriate stories of adolescents who become adults through a particular rite or deed. A group
   or individual may wish to create and move through their
   own pubescent rite of passage. With just a few verbal
   cues from the therapist, such as "allow your body to
   sculpt itself as you were as a child. . .and now as you
   will be as an adult. Now move from the child position-
   pattern to those of an adult, being aware of the evolutionary process" a ritual process may be created. Or
   have a group plan and carry out or improvise their own
   ceremonial puberty dance. (Age appropriate population)

B. Maladaptive Behavior: Inability to have an adequate
   sexual relationship due to lack of resolution of the oedipal crisis.[70] In males this may show itself in a duel
   hatred and sexual attraction to women.

Dance-Movement Therapy Techniques:

Movement ritual process involving the working through
of oedipal stirrings. Here again the accomodators may
be divided into positive and negative parents. The negative parent of the opposite sex responds seductively to
the enactor-individual. In the case of a male-identified
patient, the good father responds by not permitting any
form of sexual interaction to occur with the bad mother.
Verbalizations such as "We understand your desire to
seduce your mother, but we will not allow that to happen." Father: "Only I have sexual intercourse with
your mother." A positive more age appropriate sexual
companion is often provided in this type of psychomotor
structure. Resolution comes when the enactor-individ-

---

[70] Puberty has often been called the Second Oedipal phase due to emerging sexuality and a
resurgence of interest in the parent of the opposite sex.

ual realizes that he cannot have his mother even though she may have been seductive and that a woman of his similar age is more appropriate for him. This same structure may be reversed for an electra ritual in which the bad father attempts to seduce the daughter. [71] (Pesso) (Neurotic)

Related elements: Full efforts, P-G merger, phallic and feminine rhythms, sexual identity.

4. Marriage Ritual Process

Maladaptive Behavior: Inability to sustain a lasting intimate heterosexual relationship which may show itself in difficulty in commitment (diminished use of the vertical plane) and closed shape flow. Urethral sadistic rhythms and/or quickness and free flow may dominate the individual's repertoire. Lack of an abundance of adult genital rhythms may also be apparent.

Dance-Movement Therapy Techniques:

1. Movement activities involving a symbolic ritual union between the two individuals. The rhythm and flow of which may be evolved intuitively being aware each moment of the goal of union and of what the person is feeling in relation to their own energy and the energy of their partner. The ritual terminates when they have sculpted their bodies in appropriate relation to the other. (All adult population) (See Figure 111-19)

2. Since it is important to understand that duelism is an illusion, particularly when involved in a heterosexual relationship, movement rituals involving role reversals and/or calling forth his anima (for the man) and her animus (for the woman) may be highly important. [72] At first each of the dyad may wish to move alone in this new persona, but eventually it would be important to interact and thereby gaining a total awareness of the multiplicity of the yin/yang relationship which exists. (Normal-neurotic adults)

3. Movement ritual which involves the use of stimuli such as African or Afro-Caribbean music which simulates the sexual encounter and relationship. This may take the form of fertility rites which have existed in many primal cultures. (Normal-neurotic adults)

Related Elements: Adult genital rhythms.

[71] Pesso, op. cit.

[72] Animus: (CG Tung) The archtype that is the masculine component of all women's personalities resulting from accumulated racial experiences of women with men. Anima: feminine component. (Wolman)

Figure III-19. Marriage Ritual.

116

5. Retirement Ritual Process

Maladaptive Behavior: Despair and depression are often characterized by a giving in flaccidity (hopeless, helplessness) or a tensely bound body (depression, repressed anger and a sadness) due to feelings of loss instigated through a sense of loss of oneself—one's life. Alienation and sense of separateness may manifest itself via a decreased use of shaping and a hollowed, shortened and/or narrowed torso.

Dance-Movement Therapy Techniques:

1. Movement ritual involving the tapping into and discovery of unconscious archtypal movement patterns which stem from a collective unconscious. These patterns which have a universal-infinite quality should be encouraged and allowed to develop. Learned movement patterns which were formally associated with previous personae and/or jobs should be discouraged. It is important that some individuals understand that the latter patterns are not always an integral part of their being, and that the possible sensations of loss of oneself due to loss of job identities may really be anthetical to what is actually the case, i.e., they may now, for the first time, really be availing themselves of the possibility of being who they are. (Normal-neurotic appropriate age)

2. Movement activities involving the dissolution of body ego boundaries and the encouragement of a sense of oneness and unity with the environment. Such as a group moving in a heated pool in a clump-like mass. Individuals may be carried by others. Total relaxation is encouraged as the group takes on the form of a human seaweed. (Normal-neurotic adults) Verbal cues which stimulate body relaxation and peak experiences, yoga, T'ai Chi Chuan, and other forms of movement meditation may also be suggested.

TACTILE PERCEPTUAL LEVELS OF ORGANIZATION

In order to react to and adaptively move in an environment, an individual must first be able to perceive it appropriately. If he is unable to do so either due to neuromuscular impairment and/or an environment which has not supplied an adequate amount of stimuli, the individual will be severely impeded in his attempts to learn and integrate other adaptive patterns.

Perception of tactile stimulation is one of the first avenues open to an infant. In the womb, he reacts to stimuli produced by the grosser movements of the mother, which disturb his nirvana.

After birth, the neonate continues to respond to stimulation which, for the most part, is initiated by the mother or mother surrogate. Her ministerings of her child's needs serve to build a reservoir of various tactile experiences which are recorded and responded to at an emotive level. This data affords the infant one of the basic elements needed in the process of differentiating himself first from his mother and then from the rest of his environment. Without this ability, as seen particularly with autistic children and severely regressed schizophrenics, the individual cannot perceive where his being ends and the outside world begins—a situation which renders functioning, even at the most basic level, impossible.

The importance of this adaptive pattern, however, is often not matched by the degree of interest and attention movement therapists and educators place upon it. In a strict sense it could be argued that integration of tactile perception, or of any other form of perception for that matter, is not and should not be part of the role of the dance therapist. He should involve himself solely with the client's movement patterns and leave the integration of perceptual skills to someone else.

On the surface, this argument certainly has validity; and if there were other therapists who could work with the client in this area, there would be no necessity for the dance therapist to involve himself with the particular task. However, unfortunately there are very few psychotherapists who work at this level. Since it is an area which cannot be overlooked or discarded as unimportant to motor development and the organization of adaptive levels, the movement therapist has very little choice but to attend to the area. It must also be noted that the dance therapist, among all other psychotherapists, is best equipped to handle and treat this most basic and vitally important area.

The importance of the use of tactile stimulation cannot be over-emphasized in the work of the dance therapist. Like the dancer, the major tool of the therapist is the body. It is the primary communicative device through which the therapist and his client relate and work. Stimulation of the body serves to communicate to respondent, and often to the stimulator as well, fundamental information which is imperative to the therapeutic process.

For example, the therapist may not only use tactile stimulation to aid the individual in the acquisition of this perceptual ability, but also as a diagnostic tool. He may sense if the body is tense, rigid, or lifeless. If, for example, a cold area is detected without any apparent environmental reason, it might suggest an area charged with cathected energy. A light stroke over the torso might detect a difference in body quality which would suggest a disassociation of one portion of the body from the other such as found with the "cutting off" of the pelvic area due to sexual psychopathology (Lowen). [73]

The use of physical contact and tactile stimulation in the development of interpersonal relationships is or should be obvious to every human being whether it be a hand shake from a friend, a nurturing stroke from a mother, or a caress from a lover. Because of

its direct primitive communicative nature, some psychotherapists have made use of it to relate to those individuals who might not otherwise respond. It is only natural that movement therapists utilize this method in establishing relationships with those individuals who are in need of this basic level of reassurance. A dance therapist who refuses to do so may reinforce a person's concept of himself as an "untouchable worthless creature" as well as decrease the chances of his integrating needed adaptive patterns.

Tactile Perceptual Levels of Organization

1. Tactile Recognition

This level entails the capacity to recognize or sense tac-

[73] Alexander Lowen, "Thinking and feeling," Lecture Reprint, 1967.

tile stimulation. Recognition generally takes the form of a response of some kind such as a verbal affirmation or a motor reaction.

2. Tactile Discrimination

This level involves the ability to discriminate one tactile stimulus from another. The stimuli may differ in degree of pressure, texture, temperature or area of the body as well as their emotive quality. When the latter quality is involved, the response takes the form of either approaching (with a pleasant stimulus) or withdrawing from (with a noxious stimulus). This last ability is vital to appropriate object relationship formulations and therefore cannot be overlooked.

3. Tactile Retention and Recall

This last level involves the ability to hold in memory the tactile stimulation. This entails the capacity to remember the form and quality of the stimuli as well as the previous appropriate response to it.

Related Maladaptive Behavior with Suggested Methods and Techniques for Dance-Movement Therapy

1. Tactile Recognition

A. Maladaptive Behavior: Inappropriate use of flow. For example, a body which seems to be "too flexible" often permits stimulation to pass through the outside membrane without the necessary ego control, or a body which seems to be "too rigid," due to an individual's desire to totally withdraw from reality attempting to "desensitize" his receptor system so as not to receive any cues which might bring him into closer contact with his environment.

Dance-Movement Therapy Techniques:

Dance-movement activities which make use of the qualities of tension and shape flow. (See corresponding section.)

B. Maladaptive Behavior: Difficulty or lack of adaptive response to tactile stimulation. A good example of this phenomenon is the frequent response or rather lack of response of the autistic child to the humans around him.

Dance-Movement Therapy Techniques:

1. Movement activity involving general temperotactile

120

stimulation such as with a cold cloth or ice. Sensory stimulation should at least initially harmonize with the natural rhythm of the person. If a pool is available, it should be utilized in this area. Depending on the level of the client, the therapist may wish to hold him stimulating in utero and work toward drawing him into free and independent movement in the water.[74] (All categories)

2. Movement activity involving the therapist holding the individual usually coupled by rocking. The therapist may hold the client in a nurturing, comforting manner; or, if the individual is in a hysterical or explosive state and needs to sense a stronger more securing involvement with the therapist, he may position the individual in his lap so that the client's back is to the therapist. The arms of the client are crossed and the hands held. If he is kicking, as in an uncontrolled tantrum state, the therapist may wish to wrap his legs over those of the individual. He should not be held too tightly; some degree of movement should still be allowed to take place. Gradually, the therapist should work towards drawing the high degree of motion into slower more subtle activity. Breathing should also be duplicated by the therapist and decreased slowly to a more normal rate.[75] (children, psychotic) (See Figure III, 20, p. 122.)

C. Maladaptive Behavior: Tactile defensiveness such as often due to repressed rage and fear of the stimulator as well as of his reaction to the stimulus.

Dance-Movement Therapy Techniques:

1. Activities in which the individual himself does the initial stimulation; gradually followed by the therapist becoming involved; such as: vigorous but gentle slapping or tapping of body followed by rest for sensing. (All categories)

2. Movement activities which aid the individual in releasing the suppressed rage (such as those discussed previously in Drive-Object: external investment of aggressive drive).

[74] This nurturing holding of the individual is particularly important if the patient demonstrates any signs of body image diffusion. It is best never to force anyone into this milieu as doing so could prove to have a highly damaging effect.

[75] It is important not to overuse this method, particularly when the individual is working toward ego control, or the developing ego will be damaged. A good therapist senses when it is appropriate to hold and when not to.

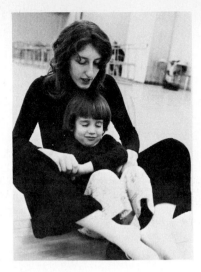

Figure III-20.

Related elements: Egocentric relationship; one-to-one or parallel group.

2. Tactile Discrimination

   A. Maladaptive Behavior: Difficulty with adaptive texture, temperature, and/or pressure discrimination. Such as a child who could not tell the difference between a smooth and rough surface.

   Dance-Movement Therapy Techniques:

   Activities involving the discrimination of various tactile stimuli involving degrees of pressure, texture, temperature or area of the body; use of cloth, brushes, sandpaper, and various other textures. For example, if the therapist were to work with the child mentioned above, she might make use of various textures of floor tiles. Graded in difficulty, she might lay out several pairs of textures and have the child while blindfolded match the pairs either by hands or feet touching the tiles. (All categories when applicable) (See Figure III, #21, p. 123.)

   B. Maladaptive Behavior: Inability to adaptively differentiate between a positive and noxious stimulus. For example, an individual who responds by growing toward a negative tactile stimulus.

122

Figure III-21. Texture Discrimination.

Dance-Movement Therapy Techniques:

Activities involving the discrimination of pleasant from unpleasant tactile stimuli by motor response. Such as those discussed in the organization of asymmetrical shape flow.

Related elements: Object dependent or object-ambivalent relationship with the therapist. One-to-one, parallel, or task group.

3. Tactile Retention and Recall

Maladaptive Behavior: Difficulty or inability in adaptively remembering the form and quality of past tactile stimulation.

Dance-Movement Therapy Techniques:

Activities involving first the stimulation of a part of the body followed, after an extendable period of time, by the individual's responses as to the area, form, and quality of the stimuli. (All categories)

Related elements: Object-ambivalent or semi-autonomous relationship with therapist; one-to-one, parallel, or task group.

123

KINESTHETIC PERCEPTUAL LEVELS OF ORGANIZATION

If the body is to move in a functional manner, an individual must be able to sense internally as well as externally. He must know unconsciously in what position his extremities are in order to make even the most insignificant purposeful movement. If he does not have this capacity he would have to watch every move scrupulously and even then his movements would be uncoordinated and perhaps athetoid in nature.

Movement of this type usually suggests certain forms of brain damage. However, if an individual is severely regressed to an infantile state or even if he has unconsciously desensitized a portion of his body, his proprioceptors and vibratory receptors may react as if there were functional impairment. The kinesthetic system is composed of the proprioceptive and vibratory senses; specifically, proprioception involves the mediation of position sense, sense of movement, deep pressure sense as well as aiding in equilibration. At least four types of receptors of this kind are located in the joints, tendons, and muscles. Their position alone justifies the attention of the movement therapist.

Vibration sense, although not as important a sense mechanism as proprioception, is still a useful detective system particularly when employed by the movement therapist.

Kinesthetic Perceptual Levels of Organization

1. Kinesthetic Recognition

   This level involves the capacity to recognize or sense proprioceptive and vibratory stimulation. Recognition may take the form of a verbal affirmation or motor reaction.

2. Kinesthetic Discrimination

   This level involves the ability to discriminate and localize proprioceptive and vibratory stimulation.

3. Kinesthetic Retention and Recall

   This level involves the capacity to hold in memory the proprioceptive and/or vibratory quality of the stimuli and to duplicate it by reconstructing the movement pattern which produced it.

Related Maladaptive Behavior with Suggested Methods and Techniques for Dance-Movement Therapy

1. Kinesthetic Recognition

   Maladaptive Behavior: Difficulty in adaptively recognizing and responding to proprioceptive and/or vibratory stimuli.

124

This could be the catatonic individual who will maintain static body positions beyond a seemingly tolerable level.

Dance-Movement Therapy Techniques:

1. Movement activities involving experience with proprioceptive recognition; such as:

    a. Activities involving the passive movement of the body or body parts followed by the individual's recognition of the movement. (All categories)

    b. While the individual has his eyes closed, ask him to duplicate various positions which the therapist has either placed the individual's body in or verbally suggested to him. (All categories)

    c. Suggest to the patient to tense and relax various parts of his body isometrically. (All categories)

    d. Activity involving the massaging of an area followed by the individual's recognition of the stimulation. (All categories)

    e. Movement activity involving resistive exercise with the therapist. For example, hold the client's hands and have him reciprocally push back and forth gradually taking the arms through a backward and forward motion while increasing the resistance. (All categories)

2. Activities involving experience with vibratory recognition; such as:

    a. Activity involving the use of hand vibrator on the body or parts of the body followed by the individual's recognition of the stimulation. (All categories)

    b. Place the individual in certain positions designed to produce vibratory coarcation of muscle bodies. After a period of time, have the individual experience these vibrations and suggest to him to allow these motions to encompass his whole body in a unified flow. (Neurotic)

Related elements: One-to-one or parallel group; egocentric, object dependent, or object-ambivalent relationship with therapist.

2. Kinesthetic Discrimination

    Maladaptive Behavior: Difficulty in adaptively discriminating or localizing proprioceptively and/or vibratorally stimulated body parts, e.g., someone who can't differentiate between his arm moving up or down.

Dance-Movement Therapy Techniques:

Movement activities involving identification of the area of the body and quality of movement based on proprioceptive and/or vibratory stimulations. For example, the therapist may take the person's arm and randomly press it gently and firmly back into the shoulder joint. The individual is asked to verbalize whether the stimulus was gentle or firm. This may of course be graded in difficulty; i.e., more subtle discriminations. (All categories)

Related elements: One-to-one or parallel group; object-dependent relationship with therapist.

3. Kinesthetic Retention and Recall

Maladaptive Behavior: Inability to hold in memory and duplicate proprioceptive and/or vibratory stimulations.

Dance-Movement Therapy Techniques:

Movement of the body either passively by the therapist or via visual iconic imitation of the therapist's movements followed, after a gradeable period of time, by the repetition of the movement by the individual. The movement may be as simple as a gesture or as complicated as a modern dance for a recital. (All categories)

Related elements: Iconic and/or enactive levels of cognition; parallel, task, or egocentric cooperative group; hobby or occupational search such as with a dance club; semi-autonomous chumship, or autonomous relationship with therapist.

VESTIBULAR PERCEPTUAL LEVELS OF ORGANIZATION[76]

As with the kinesthetic systems, adequate vestibular perception is needed in order to move in a functional, purposeful manner. Without the vestibular apparatus, an individual would be incapable of balancing. He would walk as if in a drunken stupor. No child could possibly begin to be aware of his body without the aid of this sense and its integration with other sense systems such as those mentioned in previous chapters. Likewise, an individual in a state of depersonalization can demonstrate a negation of his body which in turn affects the vestibular mechanisms producing a seemingly infantile state. [77] As described by Butter the functions of the vestibular organs located in the inner ear are as follows:

[76] The use of the vestibular apparatus in regression in the service of the ego will be discussed later.

[77] Schilder, op. cit., p. 167.

"The semi-circular canals contain receptors which respond to rotary acceleration of the head, while receptors in the utricle respond to gravitational forces on the head and to linear acceleration. Nerve fibers innervating sensory cells of the vestibular organs travel to the medulla and synapse upon neurons which go to centers controlling eye muscles and neurons in the spinal cord controlling body movement for appropriate postural reactions."[78]

Vestibular Perceptual Levels of Organization

1. Vestibular Recognition

   This involves the ability to sense vestibular stimulation. Recognition may take the form of a motor reaction such as righting oneself.

2. Vestibular Discrimination

   This involves the capacity to discriminate various vestibular stimulations.

3. Vestibular Retention and Recall

   This level involves the ability to hold in memory the vestibular stimulation and to duplicate it by reconstructing the movement pattern which produced it as well as being able to hold in memory postural positions which reestablished equilibrium.

Related Maladaptive Behavior with Suggested Methods and Techniques for Dance-Movement Therapy

1. Vestibular Stimulation

   Maladaptive Behavior: Difficulty in adaptively "catching" self or falling when individual loses balance. This could be a person who has so completely depersonalized, who wants to cut himself off from reality to such an extent that he has tried to cut off body sense systems. (To acknowledge the properties of equilibrium means also to be faced with attending to gravity and to feel "grounded.")

   Dance-Movement Therapy Techniques:

   1. Movement activities involving the production of vestibular stimulation—such activities as twirling, rolling, swinging, and other movements which cause body im-

---

[78] Charles Butter, Neuropsychology: The Study of Brain and Behavior (Belmont: Brooks/Cole Publishing, 1968), p. 108.

balance. Activities such as these serve to reintroduce an individual to his body. (All categories)

2. Passive movement activities involving the production of vestibular stimulation by the therapist, such as tilting of the individual. (All categories) (See Figure III, #22, below.)

3. Movement activities involving the use of objects which facilitate vestibular stimulation such as the use of a trampolene, balance boards, and/or tilt boards. (All categories) (See Figure III, #23, below.)

Vestibular Stimulation

Figure III-22.   Figure III-23.

Related elements: One-to-one parallel group, ego-centric, object-dependent, or object ambivalent relationship with therapist; kinesthetic recognition; gravitational efforts.

2. Vestibular Discrimination

Maladaptive Behavior: Difficulty in adaptively discriminating diverse vestibular stimulation. This could be an indi-

128

vidual who continuously over reacts by making over-compensating adjustments with each step out of an unrealistic fear of falling.

Dance-Movement Therapy Techniques:

> Passive and/or active movement activities involving the discrimination among various vestibular stimulations, e.g., tilting slightly, tilting on more of an angle. Movement activities may be graded in difficulty: for example, to facilitate the activity a mirror can be used to aid in discrimination; or to increase the difficulty, the eyes may be closed. (All categories)

> Related elements: One-to-one or parallel group; object-dependent or object-ambivalent relationship with the therapist; kinesthetic discrimination; gravitational efforts.

3. Vestibular Retention and Recall

Maladaptive Behavior: Inability to recall the movement pattern which produced a particular vestibular stimulation and/or inability to recall positions which allowed for the resumption of balance, such as a child who had difficulty remembering how to catch his balance when pushed backward.

Dance-Movement Therapy Techniques:

1. Activity involving movement of the body, either actively or passively, which causes momentary imbalance followed by the individual regaining balance. This is proceeded, after a gradeable period of time, by the repetition of the movement of the individual with emphasis on the postural positions used to regain balance. This could be done with the use of ballet positions or as a game in which the goal is to maintain one's balance during various locomotor activities such as hopping or jumping one and two legged. (All categories)

2. Duplicating of activities incorporating the use of a real or imaginary environment such as a tightrope, or a terrain which requires agile stepping. (All categories)

   Related elements: Iconic and/or inactive level of cognition, parallel group, semi-autonomous or chumship relationship with therapist.

COGNITIVE REPRESENTATION LEVELS OF ORGANIZATION

Cognition can be defined as the process through which sensory perceptions are appropriately organized such that objects and events are perceived in accordance with one's cultural group (Mosey, Ruesch, Flavell). It is, in other words, the organization of stimuli with related thought concerning that perception.

Cognitive processes then entail all mental processes concerned with knowing. One of these is the way in which perceptual-motor constructs are remembered. Without this function, no individual could benefit from experience, for each situation would be treated as unique. Its importance is obvious in the learning of adaptive behavior. A movement therapist should, therefore, be aware of the representative level at which his client is functioning in order to insure the full organization of the desired components. If he is instructing on a higher plane than the individual is capable of comprehending, the session would prove to be frustrating and purposeless. Through acknowledging the cognitive ability of the client, the therapist may then begin to aid him in the integration of higher levels of representation.

Cognitive Representation Levels of Organization[79]

1. Enactive Cognition

    This level involves the capacity to remember and reproduce a movement response through the use of physical perceptions of the movement pattern as cues.

2. Iconic-Imitative Cognition

    This level involves the ability to remember and reproduce a movement response through the use of separate pictorial images or a continuous series of images as cues.

3. Abstract Cognition

    This level involves the ability to remember and reproduce a movement response through the use of concepts, such as verbilization or dance notation as cues.

Related Maladaptive Behavior with Suggested Methods and Techniques for Dance-Movement Therapy

1. Enactive Cognition

    Maladaptive Behavior: Inability or difficulty in adaptively remembering and/or duplicating the movement response when taught at an enactive level. For example, if the girl is still unable to learn a dance step even after the teacher physically takes her through the pattern, i.e., lifts her arm and moves it in the desired way.

[79] Concepts evolved from Mosey.

Dance-Movement Therapy Techniques:

Activities involving the remembering and reproduction
of a movement response through the use of enactive
teaching. For example the therapist would passively
take the person through the desired movement pattern.
(All categories) This method is partly used in the
Alexander Technique which assists an individual in
becoming aware of and unlearning self-destructive
(maladaptive) movement patterns. This method is also
utilized in the training of dance therapists. A student
does not only listen to teacher's talking about Dance
Therapy or observe films and sessions, he or she is
involved with experiencing it, physically gets involved
in Dance and Movement, so that recall and reproduction
comes after having experienced it previously.

Related elements: Kinesthetic retention and recall;
vestibular retention and recall; egocentric, object-
dependent, or object-ambivalent relationship with therapist.

2. Iconic-Imitative Cognition

Maladaptive Behavior: Unable to adaptively imitate movements or duplicate movement from pictures. For example,
the person cannot imitate the movement of the dance therapist or other group members.

Dance-Movement Therapy Techniques:

1. Movement activities involving the use of remembering
   stimuli in terms of separate pictorial images. For
   example, the therapist may position himself in one or
   more postures such as a stance emphasizing presentation of self or communicative asking or giving which the
   patient views, after which the individual is asked to
   duplicate it. (All categories)

2. Movement activities involving the mirroring of another's
   movements. This can be graded in complexity. For
   example, the therapist and client face each other, and
   the therapist tells the person to move as he moves.
   (All categories)

3. Movement activities involving the individual duplicating
   a movement that he has just viewed. This could be a
   gesture or a sequence. The therapist may wish to make
   use of gestures, dynamics, and shape which the person
   utilizes in his own movement signature. (All categories)

131

4. Movement activities involving the duplication of movements of non-human objects. For example, the therapist could drop a scarf to the ground and ask the group to be floating scarfs. (All categories)

Related elements: Parallel, task, egocentric and cooperative group; object-ambivalent or semi-autonomous relationship with therapist.

3. Abstract Cognition

Maladaptive Behavior: Inability or difficulty in adaptively remembering and/or reproducing a movement through the use of concepts. For example, someone may be able to bend over after he has seen the therapist do it, but be unable to reproduce the pattern if only given the verbal cue of "Bend over." This might also be a person who has difficulty translating labanotation into movement even after she has been taught what they symbols mean. This same girl may be able to quickly pick up and learn a dance if she is shown the pattern.

Dance-Movement Therapy Techniques:

1. Movement activities involving the use of verbalization as a stimulus for the pattern. For example, making use of movements which the therapist has seen the person do, he might suggest some of these verbally to the person. This can be graded first by telling the person and showing the pattern simultaneously several times so that an association is made, followed by the verbal cue alone (all categories when age appropriate).

2. Dance activities involving use of a verbal imagery and abstract concepts; for example, asking the individual or group to move in response to words such as, freedom, anger, joy, sadness, etc. (all categories when age appropriate).

3. Movement activities involving the use of a notational system. For example, have an individual or group make up a dance, notate it in some written fashion, and then, after a period of time, reproduce the work from the notation (all categories when age appropriate).

Related elements: Use of play-work: hobby or occupational search; task or egocentric-cooperative group; semi-autonomous, chumship, or autonomous relationship with therapist.

THOUGHT PROCESS LEVELS OF ORGANIZATION

One of the most important areas in which movement therapists can play a major role is the evolving of an individual from a solely primary process to that of reality-stressed secondary process orientation. Since the primary process level is often characterized by symbolic nonverbal behavior (an area which is often foreign to the verbal-oriented psychiatrist or psychologist) the dance therapist may be one of the few on the team who can actively involve the patient in psychotherapy. Because of the specialized training in body language, he may understand what the patient is trying to say—a fact which is always a comfort to a struggling, confused, and often frightened human being. [80]

Thought Process Levels of Organization

1. Primary Process Thought

   This level involves the maintenance of knowledge and thought processes on an unconscious level. Archetypal[81] and idiosyncratic symbolism prevails along with an anaclytic narcissistic relationship with the environment and disregard for properties of weight, space, and time. The individual is said to be guided by the pleasure principle (Freud). [82]

2. Secondary Process Thought

   This level involves the maturation of cognition and is used in the ordering of conscious mental content. The individual is able to differentiate himself from his environment and relate to persons in a nondependent manner. Awareness and functional use of the qualities of weight, space, and time is also characteristic of this level. The individual is now also guided by the reality principle (Freud).

3. Tertiary Process[83]

   This stage involves the conscious awareness and discrimination between material which is derived solely from the unconscious, partially from the unconscious and partially from the conscious level, and/or solely from the conscious

[80] At this basic level it is also sometimes necessary to utilize one's own unconscious in order to better understand and relate to an individual utilizing primary process thought. In this way the therapist can more accurately sense the appropriate length of time needed by the patient to understand this strange "underworld" of repressed symbolized material (Sullivan, Rosen, Searles, Laing, Sesahahye).

[81] Carl Jung, Man and His Symbols (New York: Doubleday & Co., 1964).

[82] Mosey, op. cit., p. 15.

[83] Ann Mosey, Three Frames of Reference for Mental Health (Charles Block, 1970), p. 51.

level. Along with the integration of this skill comes creativity in its purest form, unincumbered by the need to perpetuate neurotic or psychotic movements. At this level the "bridge"[84] between the conscious and the unconscious is open, allowing free flow of psychic energy.

Related Maladaptive Behavior with Suggested Methods and Techniques for Dance-Movement Therapy

1. Primary Process

Maladaptive Behavior: Predominance of solely neutral flow, such as in catatonia.

Dance-Movement Therapy Techniques:.

1. Movement activities involving use of symbolic imagery and movements; such as a movement sequence which involves the individual working himself out of a small dark tunnel. (All categories)

2. Movement activities which help the individual journey into his unconscious primary process world (Sullivan, Fromm-Reichman, Searles, Gill, Laing, Hoing). The individual himself is often the best catalyst as he can supply dreams and fantasies which are meaningful to him. These symbolic processes can be enacted or re-enacted in movement dramas. Each character as well as meaningful (symbolically charged) objects should be played out by the individual. Completion of the dream or fantasy can also be crucial to conscious integration of unconscious material (Gestalt) (Adult, neurotic, children).

Related elements: Flow of breath; symmetrical shape and tension flow; flow rhythms, one-to-one group; egocentric relationship to therapist.

2. Secondary Process

Maladaptive Behavior: Inadaptive use of archetypal and idiosyncratic symbols in lieu of reality oriented secondary process thought. For example, movements; e.g., bizarre gestures, mannerisms as well as possible verbalizations which are not understood by one's cultural group due to their unconscious origin.

---

[84] Jung, op. cit.

Dance-Movement Therapy Techniques:

1. Activities stressing the use of reality oriented movement patterns with reflective verbalization. The therapist may wish to involve the person in very simple activities such as catching a ball, standing, sitting, and sensing his body in relationship to general environmental variables.

2. Use of reality based imagery such as playing ball. (All categories)

3. Activities involving establishing eye contact; such as, a game in which the therapist and child take turns trying to look in the other's eyes while the other tries to avoid contact. (All categories)

B. Maladaptive Behavior: Difficulty or lack of adaptive functional use of weight, space and time as demonstrated by a poor effort-shape repertoire.

Dance-Movement Therapy Techniques:

Activities involving the awareness and functional integration of movements requiring the use of qualities of weight, space, and time (use of all pre-efforts, directional shape, effort, and shaping) within the individual's idiosyncratic behavioral repertoire (see Effort/Shape areas for further clarification and illustration). (All categories)

C. Maladaptive Behavior: Predominance of nonverbal behavior; i.e., does not verbalize when appropriate.

Dance-Movement Therapy Techniques:

Refer to Flow of Breath and Symmetrical Shape Flow. (All categories)

Related elements: Perceptual stimulation, Effort-Shape variables; Flow of Breath; Object-ambivalent relationship with therapist; one-to-one, parallel, or task group.

3. Tertiary Process

Maladaptive Behavior: Inability to discriminate primary process thought from secondary process thought.

Dance-Movement Therapy Techniques:

1. Activities involving exploration and discrimination between movements which are reality oriented involving

secondary process thought and movements which are symbolic in nature involving primary process thought. For example, involving a group in a fantasy-movement drama followed by a movement game with the end of the session devoted to talking about the felt differences. (All categories)

2. Movement activities involving unconscious material followed by verbal discussion and psychic integration of what transpired: Such as, with the use of Gestalt, Psycho-motor, and bio-energetic techniques (all categories except children).

   Related elements: Use of creative improvisations, parallel, task or egocentric-cooperative group; semi-autonomous, chumship, or autonomous relationship with therapist.

PLAY-WORK LEVELS OF ORGANIZATION[85]

Finally, movement, and more specifically, dance, as an art form, may be utilized in organizing skills needed for leisure time activities as well as for an occupation.

Before discussing the levels of this area, it should be made clear that the use of dance in this manner is generally applicable to only a small portion of patients, if any at all. This area is utilized only if the individual has an interest in movement beyond its purely therapeutic benefits and only after he has partaken of all that Dance Therapy may offer him. Because of the confusing nature of coupling therapeutic dance with social dance or dance as an art form, these two very separate areas should never be combined. It is extremely perplexing to a patient if he perceives the session as solely "social dancing" and the leader intends to do "Movement Therapy."

This final area is therefore seen as a prelude to hospital embarkation or as a weaning process by the therapist and should be utilized after the individual has organized all the major adaptive patterns he needs to function adequately in his environment.

Play-Work Levels of Organization

1. Dance as a Hobby

   This level involves the ability to make use of dance as an expressive creative tool for leisure time. This entails being able to utilize dance extemporaneously. The body, as a dancer's tool, should be sufficiently conditioned and exercised so as to insure the artistic quality needed.

[85] Adapted from Mosey.

136

2. Dance as an Occupation

This level involves the acquisition of the needed dance skills for the particular dance form of choice. Choreography, entailing the ability to creatively problem-solve, may or may not be integrated at this time.

Related Maladaptive Behavior with Suggested
Methods and Techniques for
Dance Movement Therapy

1. Dance as a Hobby

A. Maladaptive Behavior: Body insufficiently conditioned. This could be characterized by an individual who is unable to endure more than 10 minutes of dancing without exhaustion.

Dance-Movement Therapy Techniques:

Movement activities on a regular schedule designed to stretch, strengthen, increase range of motion, work on placement, dance technique and/or endurance. These sessions can be styled after traditional dance classes. (All categories)

B. Maladaptive Behavior: Difficulty in improvisational dance. This could be a person who has always directed his life according to various authority figures; e.g., parents, teachers, therapists and has a great deal of difficulty moving in a spontaneous creative manner.

Dance-Movement Therapy Techniques:

Movement activities involving dancing extemporaneously for pure self-expression or in response to cues such as music and/or a selected image. This can be graded from a gesture to a dance. (All categories)

Related elements: Semi-autonomous or autonomous relationship with therapist, all levels of all other areas.

2. Dance as an Occupation

Maladaptive Behavior: Difficulty in creative problem solving; such as someone who is unable to choreograph a dance.

Dance-Movement Therapy Techniques:

1. Choreographic problem-solving activities. For example, suggest to the individual or group to choreograph

a movement sequence involving certain criteria such as use of various levels of dynamics or one of an expressive or kinetic nature. (All categories)

2. The production of a recital to be performed for the hospital or for the community by the individual or group. (All categories)

   Related elements: Semi-autonomous or autonomous relationship with therapist; all levels of other areas.

CHAPTER IV

Regression in the Service of the Ego

"The general assumption is that under certain conditions the ego regulates regression, and that the integrative functions of the ego include voluntary and temporary withdrawal of cathexis." Kris[1]

Occasionally it is necessary to make use of movement techniques of regression in order to facilitate the therapeutic process in the learning of adaptive levels of organization. This procedure is indicated with the individual who has fixated at the pre-genital level of development due to inadequate integration or organization of a level or phase (Freud, Whiting[2]). Although this person continues to evolve into maturity, the faulty learning at an earlier age may predispose him to a behavior disorder when stressful situations arise[3] (Erikson, A. Freud[4]).

[1] Ernst Kris, Psychoanalytic Explorations in Art (New York: Schocken Books, 1967), p. 312.

[2] John Whiting and Irwin Child, Child Training and Personality (New Haven Yale University Press, 1953).

[3] These so-called stressful situations generally bear some relationship to the initial level and etiology of the inadequate development.

[4] Anna Freud, op. cit., on Regression and Fixation:

"Most closely studied in analysis is temporal regression in drive and libido development. What is affected here, on the one hand, is the choice of objects and the relations to them, with consequent returns to those of earliest significance and the most infantile expressions of dependence. On the other hand, the drive organization may be affected as a whole and reverting to earlier pregenital levels and to the aggressive manifestations coordinated with them may be brought about. Regression in this respect is considered as based on a specific characteristic of drive development, namely, on the fact that while libido and aggression move forward from one level to the next and cathect the objects which serve satisfaction on each stage, no station on the way is ever fully outgrown, as it is on the organic side. While one part of the drive energy is on a forward course, other portions of it, of varying quantity, remain behind, tied to earlier aims and objects, and create the so-called fixation points (to autoerotism and narcissism, to the stages of the infant-mother relationship, preoedipal and oedipal dependency, to oral pleasures and oral sadism, to anal-sadistic or passive-masochistic attitudes, phallic masturbation, exhibitionism, egocentricity, etc.). Fixation points may be caused by any type of traumatic experience, by either excessive frustration or excessive gratification on any of these levels, and may exist with different degrees of awareness and consciousness or repression and unconsciousness attached to them. For the developmental outcome this is less important than the fact that for whatever cause and in either state they have the function of binding and retaining drive energies and that thereby they impoverish later drive functioning and object relations.

"Fixations and regressions have always been regarded as interdependent.[8] By virtue of their very existence and according to the measure of libido and aggression with which they are cathected, the fixation points exert a constant retrograde pull on drive activity, an attraction which makes itself felt during all early development and in maturity." Pp. 95-96.

Referrals generally occur after the "stressful situation" has transpired; however, more and more, movement therapists have been acting on a prophylactic level, treating the so-called normal neurotic. Whether the therapist comes in contact with his client before or after a disrupting event is not as important a factor as is the therapist's ability to recognize an individual with an unstable foundation.

The role of the movement therapist, then, is to (1) observe the movement repertoire of the individual, (2) determine at what level inadequate learning occurred, (3) regress the individual to the initial level of malfunction; and (4) utilizing all the necessary components from the appropriate levels of organization, provide an environment in which the individual can integrate those adaptive patterns which are needed in a functioning movement repertoire.

There are those, to be sure, who would feel it unnecessary to reproduce—even at a symbolic level—the initial environment at which the adaptive behavior should have been integrated or organized. "Let's work in the 'here and now.'" Why not just analyze the pure movement pattern which is required and teach it to the person in need? Superficially, this proposition seems to demonstrate validity. However, one has only to try it out to see how quickly it fails. For example, it is certainly more difficult to teach a person how to swim if he does not have an opportunity during the learning process to experience water. The "pure movement pattern" is not the only element needed in the learning of this skill; the appropriate environment must also be available. Without an experience in a body of water, the lack of the very basic but crucial familiarity with its qualities, would render the learning process highly inadequate.

Like the above analogy, there are basic crucial components which are needed in order for an adaptive pattern to be fully integrated or organized. Therefore, a "total movement activity" creating a "total environment" is required. It should also be noted that by "total environment" the internal as well as external environment of a client is taken into consideration. It is up to the therapist to facilitate the appropriate internal setting for the organization of the ability. It is this last area in which regression is most needed, i.e., as a tool to bring about the appropriate psychic state. An individual cannot be expected to integrate appropriately the egocentric level of the dyadic constellation if he is attempting to function on an emotional level which required autonomous interactions with the therapist.

Some may continue to dispute the use of regression stating that even though an individual is not functioning on a totally integrated manner, he nonetheless can get by. Some even feel that anyone who involves himself in such a process would demonstrate that his ego boundaries are weak and ineffectual. To some the behavior of this person would be labeled more maladaptive than someone who rigidly refuses this process in spite of his need. There are many more, however, who feel as Gill, Brenman, Laing, and Klein do: "Regression in the service of the ego is evidence of a 'strong,' not a 'weak' ego, or probably more correctly, it is evidence of an ego which has the capacity to regress in part while the depth and duration of the regression are controlled by the ego as a whole."

Movement as a Regressive Tool

Movement for obvious reasons lends itself beautifully to a regressive process. Meerloo states, "the sharing of gestures, movements, and feelings brings man back to the blessed state of dependency and togetherness which he had to relinquish in the process of growing up and becoming an individual." He goes on to point out the early biologic roots of dance, stating that in his clinical practice he has experienced dance students who used their "dance aspirations as a means to return unobstrusively to frustrated desperate moods carried over from childhood." He sites the use of dancing to rock music as a regressive tool of the young. Paul Schilder has often mentioned that through movement comes a departure from the typically rigid state to a more loosened and dissolved state such that the body is then able to return to one of the primary attitudes. [5]

The psycho-physiological process of regression may be described as a sensing that the body ego is slipping away from one's ego control. Distal extremities go before medial, caudal before cephalo, and the less sensitive, less charged areas before the erotogenic zones, areas laden with libidinal energy. [6] Disassociation often sets in with the loss of coordinated functioning. A predominance of more primitive drive-charged rhythms appear in their pure form; urethral, then anal, then oral rhythms take over the body. Utilization of effort-shape variables is virtually nonexistent, only tension flow and shape flow remains.

Or it can be described in a different manner as does Gunther in his Sense Relaxation: "Letting go/open to effortless ease/not trying; flow/to relax, release, releasing/optimal tonus. A way to allow direct experience/a return to primary process/unfiltrated contact with what is going on without expectation/or excessive inhibition/being in the now/oneness in this happening moment."

[5] Schilder, op. cit., p. 207.
[6] Paul Federn, M.D., Ego Psychology and the Psychosis (New York: Basic Books, 1952), p. 29.

A regressive movement can be initiated in any one of a number of ways. Increased strength of instinctual impulses, change in the apparatus available to the ego for adaptive functioning, and/or alteration in the external situation are three main avenues that will be discussed in this chapter. [7]

I. Increased Strength of Instinctual Impulses—is the most widely used among professionals in Movement Therapy. Some examples of this type are:

1. Anal Level Regression

   a. Movement activity involving a temper tantrum state. While lying prone on a mat or bed, the individual is asked to kick the mat with the back of each leg, alternating both legs; the arms with both hands making fists should also be hitting the mat alternating as well. [8] If the exercise is physically integrated, the head will begin to move from side to side in rhythm with the rest of the body movement (Lowen). (See Figure III, #7, p. 71.)

   b. Hitting a pillow, bed, or punching bag with gesture-posture merging while yelling, "no," "I won't," or "leave me alone."

2. Oral Level Regression

   a. Movement activities involving the person lying prone on a mat with his arms extended in the air. The person is then asked to call for his mother (or father) in the manner in which he would have as a child (Lowen). (See Figure IV, #1, p. 143.)

   b. Movement activities involving the rocking of the individual in a fetal position by another using oral libidinal rhythms while attending to his primal needs (egocentric relationship).

II. Change in the apparatuses available to the ego for adaptive functioning. The primary apparatuses are motor, sensory, and memory (Rappaport). Some examples of this type are:

1. Movement activities involving the use of spinning without spotting. Dizziness is often accompanied by regressive depersonalization since both have the same psychic nucleus (Schilder).

---

[7] Jesse Gorden, ed., Handbook of Clinical and Experimental Hypnosis (New York: MacMillan Co., 1967), p. 294.

[8] It is important to note here that arms and legs should also be in opposition when hitting the mat, e.g., (R) arm (L) leg.

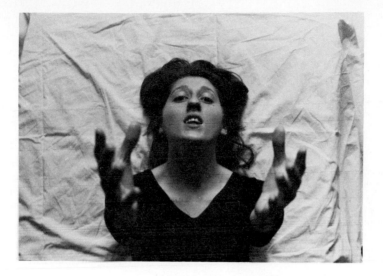

Figure IV-1.

2. Desensitization of the individual through swaddling, eyes are kept closed with a minimum of auditory stimulation. Individual may be rocked in an oral rhythm.

III. Alteration of the external situation—(It is difficult at best to separate this area out from the other two, particularly #II. Techniques are generally a combination of all three with emphasis in different areas.) However, some examples which seem to emphasize this aspect are:

1. Movement activities involving the use of a heated pool. The water can become the warm amniotic fluid of the womb to an individual who is held loosely in a fetal position by another. The eyes should be closed and the ears submerged if at all possible. The movement takes the form of the breath pulse of the individual who is holding the client. A group can also be used. Each member holding on to part of the individual's body.

2. A similar group configuration is the familiar group rock in which one member is picked up prone by the group and rocked at their waist level. Members often hum a lullaby. (See Figure IV, #2, p. 144.)

Most other methods are too difficult to separate out and classify in these three areas. One of the most common approaches centers around the sensory regressive technique in which the therapist assumes the role of a verbal facilitator guiding the individual or group back to a primary state. The voice is almost monotone,

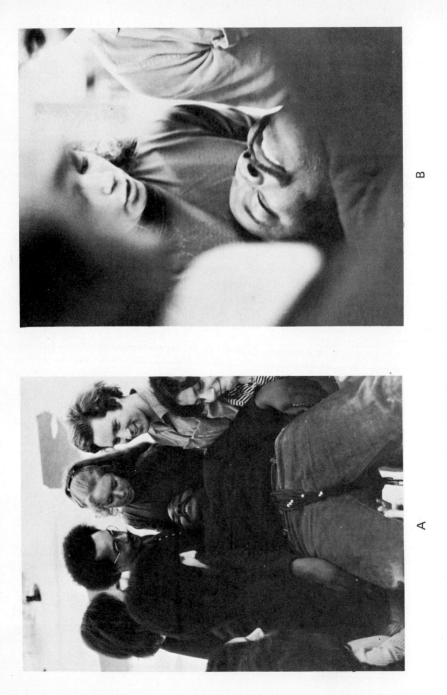

Figure IV-2. Group-Individual Rocking.

144

hypnotic and follows the breath pattern of the group. Evenness of breath, relaxation of tension, and loosening of ego boundaries producing a merging with the environment is stressed.

"The Heep"

There are other methods in which the therapist's role is solely that of initiator and observer-care taker. One which I feel is an excellent technique is what I have named "the heep." It is valuable not only as a regressive technique but also as a diagnostic tool to determine both the individual and group level of fixation. I have used this solely with groups although it can easily be adapted to individual treatment with the involvement of the therapist in a "dyad heep." The verbal stimuli for the group is:

"I would now like you to silently choose a place on the floor and form a clump or a heep such that everyone is at least touching one other member. You may lie, sit, stand—whichever seems most appropriate to you. (Group forms a heep.) Now relax, close your eyes, and get into yourself, and listen to your body. If you feel like moving do so whether it is by yourself or with other members of the group. If you feel like maintaining your position throughout this experience, that is o. k. too. There may be times you may feel bored, that too is o. k. Just listen to your body and do what you want to do. I ask only that if you wish to communicate with another that it be on a nonverbal level. This experience will be completed when everyone has stopped moving." (See pp. 146-148.)

The lights are then dimmed and music which has little or no dynamic changes—changes which might infringe upon the mood state of an individual—is played. Indian music, chants, or music from the impressionist period has been used.

Diagnostically what has been observed is that individuals in this exercise will recapitulate human development and; if there are any holes in adaptive patterns integration, they will fixate at those levels. For example, the observer may see one person move off from the group and rock by himself while another can be seen groping around the group in attempts to find someone who is moving in an oral rhythm, while another is seen continually forcing his own movement patterns on others.

If a group is a truly cohesive and functioning unit, they will be seen moving together in a unified and varying rhythm. They will also eventually be "off the ground" and moving through space. (See pp. 146-148.)

Recapitulation and Summary

Recapitulation takes place when (1) the level of fixation is ascertained and (2) the needed primal adaptive levels are integrated

The "Heep"

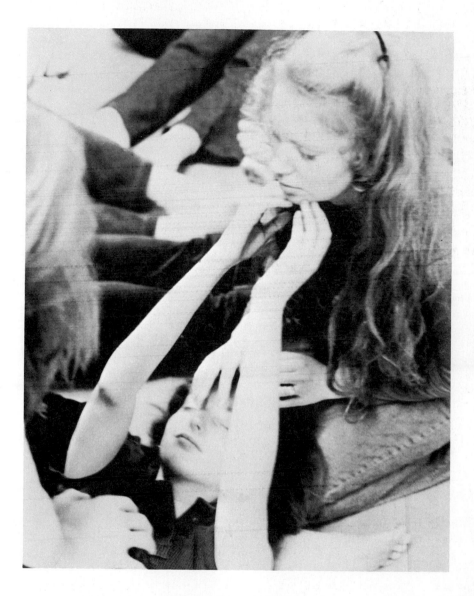

The "Heep" (continued)

The "Heep" (continued)

or organized. Quite often the recapitulation process is a natural result of the resolution of these primitive conflict areas. In any case regression is frequently a necessary tool. When it is used not as an escape mechanism but rather, "in the service of the ego"; it becomes a vehicle in which the movement therapist can evolve his client to a stronger, healthier level of functioning.

CHAPTER V

Somatatization of Symbols

Regardless of physical or psychic state, unconscious symbolic functions may be continuously active in the body attitude and movement repertoire of any person. The symbolic process may take the form of a tense body part, dead spot, pained area, body posture, or seemingly unobtrusive gesture or postural movement. The rationale and development of these symbolically charged areas varies among individuals, their experiences, and their predisposition to somatatize symptoms of psychic disfunction. One avenue is through parental and/or peer attitudes toward parts of the body and their functioning. In this case, the body-image equipped with symbolic cathexis evolves through experiencing and integrating the thoughts and actions of those in the environment.

The body is often seen as the "screen" of the ego upon which the individual projects feelings about himself and the world. Illnesses, operations, and accidents are also said to leave permanent psychosomatic tension spots which are laden with symbolism. Generally it is felt, however, (particularly in the case of tension areas), that this process is due to conflict directly related to one or more of the functions of a particular part. Lowen states, "the correlation between muscle tensions and inhibition is so exact that one can tell what impulses or feelings are inhibited in a person from a study of his muscular tensions."[1] In other words, the desire to do an act (utilization of solely agonist muscles) is counteracted by fear, guilt, double-bind, etc., (utilization of antagonist muscles as well), thus producing a tense body or body parts. Too much rigidity leads then to compulsiveness around conflict areas. (The opposite, too much flaccidity, leads to impulsiveness with possible suicidal ideation (Lowen, Rothstein).[2]

Along with symbolism placed in body parts, is the symbolic investment of certain movements. Felix Deutsch, mentioned earli-

[1] Alexander, M.D., "Breathing, Movement, and Feeling" (reprint, 1965), p. 27.

[2] Do not confuse these symptoms with the spasticity caused by CNS dynsfunction or flaccidity caused by muscular or peripheral neuropathy illnesses.

er, designed a method of "analytic posturology" which traces and evaluates the symbolism in certain motor behavior.

The symbolic process often carries with it an extra rasion d'etre which can be regarded as a somatatized defense mechanism. Tension areas usually produce "dead spots" which aid in the blocking or repression of the conflict areas. Compulsive movements which serve as undoing, compensating, or regressive mechanisms are also another example of this phenomenon.

Some Examples of Symbolic Body Part Investment

(Reich, Schilder, Lowen, Allport, Kubie,

Deutsch, Machover, Urban, Christensen)

Eyes

—"windows of the soul"

—felt to reveal inner feelings

—half closed or downward gaze:

reluctance to view the world due to possible hostility toward others

—symbolizes opening through which the environment can wander in

—incorporative attitudes, one who is afraid of being incorporated

—straining: wanting to see through everything

—tension due to inhibition of peri-occular muscles: desire to hold back crying

Nose

—symbol of sexuality and power strivings

—continuous snorts: primitive aggression

—tension due to fear of breathing in poision, radar, gas, etc., (Paranoidal ideation)

—continuous shallow sniffs: fear of taking in or letting go

Mouth, Teeth, and Jaw

—mouth emphasized; oral eroticism

—tense: refusal to reveal self

—tense: rejection of dependent needs

—teeth clenched: oral aggressiveness

—teeth clenched: biting sarcasm

—tension: inhibition of crying and sadness

—tension: inhibition of anger

—tension: fear of taking anything in e.g., an expressed thought or feeling of another

—inhibition of biting impulses

Neck, Throat

—hypertonus of neck: displaced genital anxiety

—tension: something "can't be swallowed"

—tension: something or someone who is a "pain in the neck"

—tension: a means of cutting off body emotions which have been in the heart or gut area

—tension: a means of insuring lack of intellectual or conscious awareness of feelings placed in the body i.e., the head is cut off from his body

—tension: fear of being struck from behind

—tension: fear of screaming out

—tension: fear of losing one's head

Shoulders, Arms and Hands

—provide strength and power and indicates power strivings

—depressed: an attempt to hold back aggression, holding from striking out

—raised: fear, scared stiff

Arms are instrumental in:

"handling" the world

rejecting others

reaching out to or pushing away others

aggressing or defending oneself

carrying out operations

—tension: fear or guilt over hitting out

—hands: tools for manipulating environment

—weak hands: arms: inadequacy feelings

Chest, Stomach

—pain: suppression of sadness—longing

—queasy: can't stomach something

—tension: repression of sadness

—tension: repression of anger

—conflict between infantile oral craving and super-ego adult rejection

Pelvis and Genitals[3]

—tension and blockage of flow: denial of sexuality

—tension and blockage of flow: fear of castration

Back

—backache syndrome: on guard wavering between fight and flight

—tension: inability to mobilize his anger to overcome frustration

—lordosis: sexual inadequacy[4]

—tension: something or someone is on his back

—tension: fear of being ganged up upon or carrying on behind his back

Buttocks

—tension: fixation at the anal stage

—"tight ass": fear of losing inner parts of the body

—"tight ass": fear of anal castration

—"tight ass": latent or overt homosexuality

—tucked: like a dog with his tail between his legs

Legs and Feet

Symbolic of degree of support, balance, mobility and thus an individual's sense of autonomy

—broad stance: defiance of authority

—broad stance: denial of insecurity

---

[3] Other parts of the body which protrude such as the nose, foot, etc., may also serve as substitute phallic zones with similar rationales for symbolic investment.

[4] Do not confuse this or any other symptoms with those of purely physical etiology, e.g., congenital lordosis. A working knowledge of medical conditions and surgical procedures with resulting physical disabilities is imperative. Occasionally patients have been referred for dance psychotherapy when the cause of their symptom(s) is physical in nature.

154

—legs closely pressed together: self-conscious, resistive to sexual advances

—tonicity: dependent often on genital drives and conflicts

—feet placement represent individuals grasp of reality e. g. light tenuous: on tiptoes or clutching: toes digging into ground

—tension: conflict between guilt or fear and the desire to kick out

—dead feeling: doesn't feel like he can stand on his own two feet

—dead feeling: doesn't feel grounded

Gestures

There are countless examples of symbolic gestures which can be either interpreted universally or idiosyncratically. These processes depend on many factors; among them: (1) the inherited predisposition, (2) sequences of experiences and the relationship placed upon them, (3) the original fixational situation of a gesture, (4) original response made to a stimuli, and (5) the specific symbolic element in the situation, [5] (6) as well as the cultural disposition. [6]

G.W. Allport states that:

"Much behavior in the young child is sinkinetic; that is to say, his adaptive acts are accompanied by auxiliary movements. This seems to be a natural stage in the process of transition from adjustment with single limbs. In fact Oseretzky finds these "Mitbewgengen" a serviceable index of inferior motor development. Sometimes, as Holt has shown, vestigial infantile movements persist throughout life and become motor idiosyncracies of the individual. Many of these idiosyncracies, of course, are quite specific and persist as 'symbolic gestures'; but they are at the same time further evidence that adult expression is not completely specialized or entirely free from early ties." [7]

Symbolic Body Expressions

It might be appropriate here to mention the many examples of the use of expressions which disclose the symbolic investment in the body.

[5] Maurice Korut, "A Preliminary Note on Some Muscular Responses of Diagnostic Value in the Study of Normal Subjects," American Journal of Psychiatry, II (1931-1932), p. 65.

[6] Ibid., p. 38.

[7] Allport, op. cit., p. 19.

Head

—head on your shoulders

—leads with his chin

—biting personality

—stiff upper lip

—headstrong

—loses his head

—head in the clouds

—pain in the neck

—stiffnecked

—facing the challenge

Anterior Torso

—heart ache

—cold hearted

—lump in my throat

—gutless—has no guts

—gut response—gut level

—no stomach for it

—makes him sick to his stomach

—he's got no balls

Posterior Torso

—cold shoulder

—spineless

—yellow streak down his back

—tight ass

Legs

—weak kneed

—not a leg to stand on

—cold feet

—pushover

—feet on the ground

—gets a kick out of it

—can't get off the ground

—stands up for what he believes in

More general expressions:

—scared stiff

—strung out

—fly into a rage

—out of it (out of his head)

—being big or being small

—psyched out

—up tight

—disconnected

—being together

—up in the air

—good vibrations

—hang loose

—unglued

—he's all over the place

—like a machine

—soul

—shiftless, itchy, slippery, dizzy

—natural rhythm

Therapeutic Process

No symbolic investment of body parts, gestures, or phrases which the individual uses should go unnoticed or unutilized in the therapeutic process. These, when detected, can serve as invaluable data, particularly in determining the level of dysfunction. For example, a tightened buttocks: level of fixation 1-1/2 - 2-1/2 years (see p. 65), or a rhythmic gesture repetitively stroking an object, twirling hair, or fingering the mouth: level of fixation 0 - 1-1/2 years.

Always ask the individual in question what the tension spot, gesture, pain, etc., means to him. All to often the person is overlooked and a highly idiosyncratic process is misinterpreted.

This dialogue cannot occur, however, until the symbolic process is brought into conscious awareness of the person. There are many ways to bring this about. One of the most widely used methods is to put the person into positions in which he feels his tension (Lowen). [8] Another is through physical manipulation of the area (Reich, Rolf). Another is through sense relaxation with explicit verbalization of here and now awareness (Gestalt-Perls). Another is through the realization of the person's inability to perform certain movements in a coordinated fashion. Another is by having the person view himself in a mirror, video-tape, or by his palpitating his body to feel the "cold spots."

Regardless of the method used, this very important area must be dealt with in therapy. No matter which levels of organization or what areas are being centered upon, the utilization of the symbolic process transforms the therapy into a "total movement activity." [9]

[8] See Flow of Breath.

[9] The symbolic process can be utilized in the verbal imagery, in the centering on a particular body part to be worked on, or in the acting out and working through in movement.

CHAPTER VI

The Impact of Culture on Movement
Behavior and Movement Therapy

The viewing of an individual's movement repertoire from solely a developmental-psychiatric standpoint without consideration of the cultural manifestations is a miopic and dangerous proposition (as dangerous, I might add as its reverse). All too often dance therapists look at motor behavior in terms of the presence or absence of pathology, the degree of physical and psychic integration, or the adaptability of the movement behavior without any thought as to the cultural implications. Compounding this is the fact that many of the above indicators are culturally biased—not to mention the effect of the therapist's own cultural patterns.

It is important that all clinicians take their heads out of the sand and view individuals and groups in a wider context. If these people are to rehabilitate an individual, an awareness of the movement patterns that are culturally and economically significant for him are imperative. All too often, resocialization or therapy means the unsuccessful attempt of one group, one level of society, to channel another group into a stereotyped automaton of themselves.

People from different cultures and sub-cultures move differently. Weston La Barre in his study of the cultural basis of movement has proven that there is no "natural" universal language of emotional gesture and that gesture tends to be culturally determined.[1] Birdwhistle revalidates La Barre's results and further states that these movement patterns are "kinesthetic languages" which are learned by members of a culture as is the usual verbal method of communication.[2]

Recently, Alan Lomax in conjunction with Irmgard Bartenieff and Forestine Paulay compiled a study utilizing a cross cultural analysis of movement parameters of fifty cultures.[3] From the

[1] Weston La Barre, "The Cultural Basis for Emotions and Gestures," Journal of Personality, 16, 1947, p. 67.

[2] Ray Birdwhistle, Introduction to Kinesics, (University of Louisville, Michigan, 1967), xerography, p. 65.

[3] Alan Lomax, Folk Song Style and Culture, (Plimpton Press, Washington, 1968).

many observations they were able to state: "The way that the present parameters sorted themselves out from a great number of often most abstract subtilties during our research has convinced us that these descriptions of movement behavior actually extract the essential characteristics which differentiate different areas of humanity from another."[4]

The regions of culture-movement were reconfirmed by their folk song style. But of more relevance is the fact that after studying the movement qualities of the "main activity patterns of everyday life and their functions as a means of reinforcing and supporting the principal survival patterns of the culture" it was found that the movements required for the above manifested themselves in other areas of the culture such as at play and particularly in their dance style. This study has further shown that the main determinents of movement style variation seem to be the type of economy and the level of its complexity. Similarities of movements of individuals when not at work are drawn between various cultures who have the same type of subsistence economy.

Culturally determined social sanctions, government, degree of stratification, male-female interaction, and social relationships were also found to influence an individual's movement patterns. Movement, and dance specifically, has served as a training mechanism in the integration of various cultural elements. For example, anthropologist, Judith Hanna states, "African dances become meaningful and important in terms of their function as sources of cultural indoctrination, social control, and communication."

What does all this have to do with movement therapy? The jungles of Africa may seem far away from clinical settings. It is, however, quite relevant. This pure and relatively untouched dance style affords us an opportunity to view the use of movement without the complication of a "melting pot" society such as would be found in the United States or, for that matter, in a large part of the Western Hemisphere.

Movement Analysis of Cultural Patterns

The study of African movement styles as a comparison will also allow us to trace the ancestry of blacks who live in the U.S. Naturally there are differences within the total African profile, there are different subsistence economies, geography, etc. However, there are some easily traceable similarities which aid in the differentiation of European—American-European movement styles from that of Negro African and Afro-American.

[4] Irmgard Bartenieff, "Research in Anthropology: A Study of Dance Styles in Primitive Cultures," CORD, Research in Dance, May 1967, p. 103.

One of the most differentiating elements is that of body attitude. The Negro primarily uses his trunk as a two-unit system, contrasting movement can be seen in the upper and lower halves of the trunk; whereas, the one-unit system dominates the European (and Asian) population. [5] This factor alone can have a large effect on the diagnosis and treatment of individuals in these two continents.

Compounded with this is the discovery that Afro cultures generally utilize wider effort/shape variations than the European population. Blacks also rate higher in the use of flow[6] than do white European-Americans demonstrating more spontaneity and less ego control of their movement (Kestenberg).

W.C. Condon has filmed whites, blacks, and black-white interactions to sort out, among other factors, the degree of movement synchrony between dyads. There appears to be more movement synchrony between white dyads and black dyads with much less in black-white communication. Condon also speaks of a "beautiful rhythmic pattern" between the black dyads which, when this author observed, seemed to entail a large loading of synchronized flow attributes.

(It might also be important to note here that many Negroes have experienced much use of movement as a form of expression from early childhood, and may, therefore, feel more comfortable with its use.)

There are subtle European variations which also should be taken into consideration when working with different groups. Shape flow design is one of the major cultural indicators, (Kestenberg). For example there is a larger proportion of wide reversals into reach space (kinesphere) with Italians than with the French or English. There are differences within each country as well. The shape flow of the southern French, for example, seems to be a composite of northern French and Italian patterns.

To describe all the intricacies and tones of cultural and subcultural movement styles is not the purpose of this book or even this chapter. It would take a book in itself to come even close to this proposition. Rather, this author hopes only to draw the reader into a deeper awareness of and respect for the many parameters which are present.

Sorrowfully, very little work has been done in the study of the U.S. —most being done in the observation of more "pure" cultures. The United States is a cultural mixture to be sure and

---

[5] Lomax, op. cit., p. 237.
[6] Ibid., p. 257.

movement ethnographer-notators have shyed away. The average
American is a combination of many backgrounds and multi-
environments. A good example of which is some of the white youth
today who have incorporated characteristically Afro-American
dance styles into their rock culture. The phrase, "he dances
black" is understood by most all within this subculture. Nevertheless, there are many patterns which remain and are transmitted
via the culturally biased parents to their children.

Anthropologist Ruth Benedict states in a study of child rearing
practices: "Careful studies of mother-child relations have abun-
dantly shown the infant's sensitivity to the mother's tenseness or
permissiveness, her pleasure or disgust, whether these are
expressed in her elbows, her tone of voice, or her facial expression. Communications of these sorts take place from birth on and
when a particular form of parental handling is standardized as
'good' and 'necessary' in any community, the infant has a greater
multiplied opportunity to learn the traditional patterns."[7]

Notes on Movement Therapy Application

What does all of this mean for a dance-movement therapist?
In general it means he should take all of the above into consideration
when diagnosing and establishing a treatment plan. Issues such as:
is this individual going back to his subculture to live and/or work,
or is he entering a new setting, one which requires a different
movement style if communication is to be optimum. Discussion,
films, and role playing with emphasis on NVC would be of help
here.

Ideally groups should be divided culturally as well as in terms
of adaptive pattern level.

The movement therapist should have a working knowledge of
his or her cultural movement style and be able to adapt it when
needed in order to afford greater synchrony and movement rapport
with the client.

Music which is culturally familiar to the individual often has
proven to be a comforting factor particularly if he is in strange
surroundings. Sharing a familiar song or melody with him will
establish an avenue of communication which might otherwise not be
open to you. Culturally related music may also serve to draw him
closer to his conflicts by triggering off remembrances.

If there is only one thought from all of the above which could

[7] Ruth Benedict, "Child Rearing in Eastern European Countries," Personalities and Cultures.
Robert Hunt, Ed. (New York: National History Press, 1967), p. 342.

be recalled, let it be this: No one cultural movement pattern is superior to another; movement which might be diagnosed as pathological in one country could be considered normal and even enviously desired in another. (Paulay) Miopia can not only be a maladaption of eye functioning but of perception as well. [8]

[8] Having no other related place to put this bit of information, but feeling it too important to discard; I am extracting Allport's list of "factors which may influence movement" as a gentle reminder and a prophilaxis against miopia:

1—Exigencies of immediate goal
2—Deformation of the body
3—Condition of health and disease
4—Individual peculiarities of muscular structure and body metabolism
5—Constitutional make-up
6—Age and sex
7—Strain and fatigue
8—Physical environmental conditions
9—Habits from special training
10—Racial tradition
11—Temporary social environment, leading to artificial manners or to a masking of normal expression.

CHAPTER VII

The Movement Therapist

Dance Therapy Training

The field of Dance-Movement Therapy is young and growing. It aspires to the professionalism which other forms of therapy have already attained. One of the avenues just opened in this direction is the development of graduate programs specializing in Dance and Movement Therapy. Curricula are being crystalized. Here is one example of the type of curriculum for such a program.

Prerequirements

    B. A. or B. S. degree

    Minimum of 6 credits in psychology

    Minimum of 9 credits in anthropology, sociology or education

    Minimum of 9 credits in dance (or its equivalent in studio experience)

    Anatomy and kinesiology

Core Courses in Dance Therapy	Credits
Dance Therapy Theory (2 sems.)	6
Dance Therapy Process (2 sems., self movement analysis first semester, experiental practice second semester)	4
Observation, notation, and interpretation of Movement (2 sems.)	4
Practicum (6 months full time or equivalent)	2
Thesis in Dance Therapy	2
Total	18

Psychology (Minimum of 6 credits)   Credits

    (If have not already taken must take)

    Human Development

    Abnormal Psychology

Other Suggested Courses

    Research and Statistics

    Systems of Psychotherapy

    Exceptional Children

    Child, Adolescent, or Geriatric Psychology   6

    Movement and Dance (Minimum of 6 credits)

    Modern and Creative Dance

    Folk or Ethnic Dances

    Motor Learning

    Practicum in Teaching Dance   6

6 Months Practicum   2

    Total   32[1]

Alternate Solutions to the M.A. in Dance Therapy

1. Experience in teaching creative dance to normal students

    Additional psychology courses such as abnormal psych. and psychotherapy

    Dance Therapy workshops

    Dance Therapy internship

2. M.A. in dance with a minor in psychology

    Dance Therapy workshops

    Dance Therapy internship

3. M.A. in psychology with a minor in dance

    Dance Therapy workshops

    Dance Therapy internship

4. Certificates or diplomas from overseas gymnasia, professional schools, conservatories with the same emphasis

---

[1] This curriculum meets the pending requirements of the American Dance Therapy Association for the Registry of Dance Therapy. It might also be relevant to note here that a full time Dance Therapist be on the faculty and that there should be a Dance Therapist at the field placement.

5. B.S. or M.A. in physical therapy, occupational therapy, nursing or related health profession

    Dance training

    Dance Therapy workshops

    Dance Therapy internship

6. M.D. in related speciality such as psychiatry, orthopedics, etc.

    Dance Therapy training

Movement Therapy Analysis

All the training in the world would be rendered ineffectual if the dance-movement therapist is not aware of his or her own movement repertoire and has not resolved somatitized maladaptive behavior. Areas such as:

1. Tension areas, degree of breath flow

2. Effort/shape profile

3. Flow rhythm profile

4. Posture gesture combinations

5. Dyadic and group experience

should be germaine to any analytic procedure. If the recapitulation theory is to be used, experience in all constellations should be a prerequisite to insure integration of these areas. For how, then, could an individual help another integrate an adaptive pattern if he has difficulty with that area himself. If that level is even slightly frightening to the client, he is going to be even more fearful of it if the therapist feels uncomfortable with it. Without self knowledge of these problem areas, effective patient selection and patient care would fall far short of the optimum level.

The significance of an active awareness of the therapist's cultural style has been discussed in the previous chapter. Its relevance to patient selection is crucial.

General specialty areas should be analyzed so that the dance therapist would know what population he would best facilitate. For example, if a therapist had a high effort/shape loading with minimal amounts of flow change (one who is physically competent, efficient, but not particularly spontaneous), children would not be his forte (Kestenberg). Children, of course, have far more flow—many not having integrated E/S dynamics at their level of development.

The ideal therapist, naturally, would be one who had a high loading of effort/shape attributes with a lot of flow (characterizing an individual with maturity without sacrificing spontaneity—one then, who is natural and at ease).

Hopefully if problem areas or severe impediments are discovered in a Movement Therapy analysis, the individual will seek resolution of the problems. Some have tried to conceal difficulties rationalizing that they have nothing to do with the treatment process of the patient. But this is a fallacy. Even if the problem has little relation to the problems of the client; patients, particularly those who are "severely disturbed" are often more aware of the therapist's primary process thoughts than he is himself. They know at an instant what the emotional hang-ups of those around them are, including the staff. There is nothing really mysterious about this phenomenon; it is merely that their lives are on symbolic primary process levels. They think, perceive, and react unconsciously and they are quick to receive clues around them from that level.

Some other therapists have felt that they are able to adequately move using a full repertoire of variables if needed without appropriate integration. But here again the clarity of movement fuzzes, the energy level is curtailed due to the amount of energy invested in maintaining defenses, inadequate postural integration is manifested, not to mention the many maladaptive symptoms which appear in lieu of adaptive functioning.

Movement analysis for therapists or future dance therapists when utilized properly does not become a "therapy session" per se. Granted the process may incorporate some "therapy" techniques, but the general attitudes and goals are specialized to meet the needs of a movement therapist. A group learning experience is generally the most useful, with each member giving each other feedback when involved in various experiences—be they exercises, role playing, turns in leadership or other techniques. Knowledge of one's movement repertoire can serve as a foundation upon which subtle variations can be built establishing new foundations and familiarity with hithertofore unutilized movement skills.

Notes on Supervision

The field of Movement-Dance Therapy manifests its youth in many ways. After 20 years a definition of a dance therapist is just beginning to be crystallized. However, as with all others in the health profession, the therapist as a "therapist" is just one of many roles with which he is involved particularly if he is in a clinical, institutional setting. Among these is quite often the role of supervision. Students, dance therapists, and occasionally other personnel in related areas may all at one time be supervisees.

But just what is supervision? Many feel that it means "control" over others. Some come prepared with lists of tasks and requirements which the supervisees must follow and carry out. A

168

supervisor-supervisee relationship, like the therapeutic relationship, is a mutual effort. No one person exerts his will over the other. The supervisor is a facilitator not a ruler. Responsibility is never taken away from the supervisee; he is at least 50% of the team and will gradually take over more and more of the percentage until the supervisor has "facilitated himself out of a job."

The student, then, together with the supervisor decides a plan of action for supervision with as many factors being taken into consideration as possible. For example:

1. Level of adjustment and emotional maturity

2. Level of competency in various areas

3. Appropriate patient load

4. Extra-patient treatment interests and responsibilities should be regarded carefully.

But first and foremost remember: ASK THE SUPERVISEE WHAT HE WANTS TO GET OUT OF THE RELATIONSHIP.

Generally the relationship is still patient oriented. Cases are discussed; the student or therapist may be occasionally viewed through a two-way mirror when engaged in treating.

It has been found that supervisors comment on areas for various reasons: to hear themselves talk, to prove to the student and hence to themselves how knowledgeable they are, or to facilitate growth in the supervisee. Generally when suggestions are translated into questions which seek to draw answers from the supervisee rather than direct explanation; responsibility for growth is maintained by the student while his mind is gaining experience in creative problem solving. (And, by the way, it never ceases to amaze me the amount of beautiful ideas which flow from students whose brains have not been suffocated by the ego of their teacher.)

Notes on Administration

Administration is another one of those responsibilities which seem to creep into the realm of the duties of a movement therapist. "Successful administration is the creation of an environment which enables a group of qualified people to contribute toward a socially valued purpose to the fullest extent of their individual capacities and resulting personal satisfaction, growth and fulfillment." (Group for Advancement of psychiatry.)[2]

In other words, effective administration facilitates the efficient and productive use of the staff and the facilities available. There are many ways of going about good administration, but regardless of the vehicle, planning is one of the first steps. Defining

[2] Mosey, op. cit., p. 219.

who, what, where, how, and when as well as policies, procedures, and methods are usually better decided upon before a problem arises around them. Once these areas have been explored, some type of organization, no matter how small the department, must be established. Chains of command, specific job titles and descriptions, supervision, assignments, staff development, and equipment, layout, and supplies are all areas of attention. Once these have been worked through, the Dance Therapy Department is ready to carry out its function. The administrator, then, as coordinator and supervisor facilitates avenues of communication and evaluates the effectiveness of the department.

Personnel

Administrator—responsible for the "professional performance of the department's staff as well as the planning of overall treatment policies and procedures for patient treatment programs."[3]

Staff Therapist—full or part time, his first responsibility is the patient. He is responsible to the administrator, supervisor, and physician. Duties generally consist of patient care, communication with referring physician, social worker, or any other staff related to the case, and the writing of evaluations, treatment plans, and progress notes.

Supervisor—"directs and supervises staff therapists and other subordinate personnel."[4]

Consultant—an individual who is highly qualified to give advice in a specialized field, e.g., cultural movement style variations, African dances, physical disabilities, etc.

Student Intern—the department is responsible for providing a student affiliation which meets the student's needs and the demands placed on him in his future work.

Aides, Orderlies, Attendants—in some institutions other staff members participate in the Dance Therapy experience. Communication with these individuals is imperative. It may mean the difference between a possible co-leader and an angry and confused outsider.

Physical Facilities and Equipment

Space for:

Offices

Storage of Equipment

[3] Manual on Administration (New York: AOTA, 1965), p. 22.
[4] Ibid.

Treatment Area—Many dance therapists choose to work on the floors where the patients live. Since the clients are most familiar with this area it often affords an atmosphere which is more condusive to therapy. In other situations, however, the reverse is true. Regardless, it is wise to have a room available for treatment. Even if the groups are led on the ward, individual treatment should take place in a separate room. Ideally the room should be large enough to accommodate the largest group without producing a "claustrophobic" reaction to moving in a cramped space, but not so big as to give a sense that there are no limits, no controls if needed. Acoustics, wood flooring or carpet (wall to wall so no one slips), and adjustable lighting is vital. One wall should have a large full length mirror which would be big enough for at least two people. There should also be a curtain or panel to cover it when it is contraindicated as an aid in treatment. A two-way mirror for observation is also a needed feature.

Equipment

Record Player

Records—basic records have traditionally been: waltzes, related folk (Hebrew, polkas, African, Rock, Greek, Caribbean-latin); music which doesn't superimpose its mood such as Indian, chants, or impressionistic; mood music for anger, sadness, fearfulness, joy, tranquility, feeling big, small, light, heavy, slow, quick; or music to emphasize flow or full effort actions such as flicks, dabs, glides, punches, slashes, floats, wrings, and presses. Special records which have particular meaning to the client have also been invaluable.

Percussion Instruments

Mats or Matresses

Pillows or Punching Bag

Stretch Rope or Stretch Circular Band

Towels

Wooden horse or structure to support the body when leaning over (Lowen)[5]

Other equipment will vary depending on the budget and the population. For example when working with children including those with learning disabilities, some examples of equipment would be:

Parachute

Balance Board

[5] For the releasing of tension areas in the back.

Walking Board

Trampoline

Balls

Two color materials such as ribbon (left-right discrimination)

Two color tile squares to place on the floor (foot placement with left-right discrimination)

Various modular forms (making obstacle course, imaginary scene, or stage)

Various texture floor tiles (texture discrimination)

Hulla Hoops

Weights (type that wraps around wrists and ankles)

Various objects for duplication of movement qualities such as scarfs, balloons, rock, tin foil, rubber, clay, etc.

Various fabrics, masks, hats, etc. for dramas in movement.

Regardless of the age a pool is a marvelous facility to have available; however, it is highly unreasonable to expect an institution to build one just because the Movement Therapy Department wants one. But if there is one existing, be sure to section off some time.

Clothes

Clothes, like the way a person stands and moves, send off non verbal messages to the individuals in the environment. So it is important to be sure of what you want to say! Also constant variation in clothing can sometimes have an adverse effect on a patient. To some, the environment is at best confusing. A familiar person in familiar clothing is a comforting relief. [6]

Interdepartmental Administration

The coordination of all the departments for the proper functioning of the institution is the major goal of interdepartmental administration. One of the tools which facilitates this is communication. However, major difficulties frequently arise in this area. Much communication between departments is ritualistic. [7] More often than not professionals accommodate each other's differences and show little concern or interest. Power struggles develop and those who are not comfortable with themselves and their clinical roles often get threatened easily by others particularly if it seems the "others" are more successful than they. Physicians are no ex-

---

[6] Autistic children are particularly sensitive to any change in their environment and that includes a change in his therapist's clothes.

[7] Mosey, ibid.

Stretch Band

Parachute

Figure VII-1.

ception to this either. And if the doctor is threatened by the movement therapist, the therapist is confronted with a problem.

There are many ways to handle this particular situation—one of which is not to handle it at all, which, of course, will be discarded immediately! Growth in interdepartmental knowledge of Dance Therapy as well as one's status and that of the profession can be easily stiffled by blocking this issue. If another movement therapist replaced him, he or she will have to work twice as hard to move himself out of this "defunct" position.

One way to deal with this problem is for the dance therapist to admit that he doesn't know everything and that he doesn't look to the other therapist—be he doctor, psychologist, etc.—for omniscient panaceas and solutions to all problems. Once the therapist senses the dance therapist's sharing, non-threatening, relaxed manner; perhaps he will realize that he is not expected to be "SUPERTHERAPIST" and can begin to transfer some of the energy he employs for this defense to more productive use. Perhaps, also, if a dance therapist could come to terms with some of his own anxieties (if he has any, that is), this process of communication would be much easier. In movement terms, if flow is added to his repertoire, whatever it is, a person is at least halfway there.

CHAPTER VIII

Case Studies

BETSY

Betsy was a 17-year old institutionalized adolescent diagnosed as having an adolescent depressive reaction. She was referred to the movement therapist by a psychiatrist who continued seeing her in therapy. It was decided that Betsy be seen individually once a week by the therapist.

Initial observation-evaluation in an interactional session showed Betsy to have a great deal of maladaptive behavior in the flow of breath area. Her breathing was shallow and held at times of stress. A high degree of tension was present in the jaw and mouth. Her verbalizations were tight and whispered. She seemed to alternate between a sad forlorn smile and a sustained biting of her lips.

She was able to move utilizing the various effort/shape elements; however, there was no presence of posture-gesture or gesture-posture mergers in flow or effort/shape. Puppet-like behavior with tense artificial movements replaced P-G flow in situations where the merger would cathect psychic somatized material with which she was not ready to deal. It was clear that many of her movement patterns were of an anal sadistic nature particularly in the peri-oral region making it even more difficult for her to yell out. Her negative body-image was reinforced by the intense retro-flexed rage she kept within herself. In terms of drive-object organization, her fear of letting go was also shown in her subtle passive-aggressive behavior. Cognitive representation and perceptual areas of function were all intact. The dyadic relationship commenced on a semi-autonomous level.

Betsy's self-portrait (which was also used for diagnostic purposes) showed an unhappy face scantily attached to a wavy asexual body. The phrase "she didn't have a leg to stand on" clearly applied.

Rx: Immediate Goals

1. Increase flow of breath

2. Posture-gesture flow

3. Positive affect investment with emphasis on the release and integrated awareness of retroflexed rage (Body-image, Drive-object)

Long Range Goals

1. Sexual identity stage (Body-image)

2. Increase feminine rhythms (Flow Rhythm)

3. Appropriate investment of aggressive drives (Drive-object)

4. Autonomous relationship (Dyadic)

5. Merging of P-G and G-P Effort/shape (Effort, Shape, Posture-Gesture)

The sessions often commenced with interactional movement patterns evolving into use of a strong, quick, direct pattern. Trust developed when Betsy was allowed to work through her pent up anger in psycho-motor situations in which the therapist would cower in defeat as the aggressive object while being "destroyed" with punches, kicks, slashes, and angry verbiage. It was after these situations that Betsy was able to verbalize most freely viewing with more realism her relationship with the individual(s) in question.

Shortly after starting, Betsy began bringing in favorite records which were charged with associations for her. Many sessions were started by both she and the therapist singing and moving to Carol King's "You've Got a Friend." The singing and dancing in synchrony reiterated the content of the song and further reinforced the contract. After a while Betsy brought in dreams as well; and under the supervision of the psychiatrist, they were worked through in movement. The gestalt hypotheses of dreams was utilized, i.e., that every aspect, e.g., object, person, etc., of a dream is part of the individual himself. Through personifying various elements in her body attitude and movement, she was able to move clearly, understand the heretofore bound internal conflicts, separate the issues and emotions, and resolve them.

As she grew to feel more positively about herself, she was able to evolve a chumship level of relating to the therapist. Discussion of hair styles, clothing, and ways of relating to the opposite sex enhanced her emerging sexual identity as well as such suggestions as "How would someone dance if they didn't want to be appealing . . ." now, "How would they dance if they did want to be appealing." It was during experiencing the latter that Betsy, for the first time, willingly looked in the mirror at herself with a smile, while moving in an adaptive effort-shape gesture-posture merger to a favorite rock piece.

JIM

Jim was a five year old diagnosed as having an adjustment reaction. In his case, he was seen solely by the movement therapist in individual sessions. Jim's initial evaluation was through a two-way mirror giving the therapist an opportunity to notate using an adapted Kestenberg Movement Profile. [1]

Pre-effort/Directional Shape

Jim was continually acting suddenly, but showed very little intensity in his actions. Gentleness was the primary pre-effort utilized and was coupled frequently with suddenness. Little or no pre-effort investment was placed in exploring or communicating; he would seem to act before examining or clarifying his feelings. When the pre-effort graph is compared with that of the directional shape, the obvious dissimilarity between the corresponding elements denotes in Jim's case that he reacted like a "shot gun" with no intention as to where his movement was to be directed. Directional shape was primarily in the vertical. Although he seemed to exhibit a good deal of downward movements, there was little or no correspondence in pre-effort dynamic attached to it. He seemed to have his "head in the clouds" rather than "his feet on the ground." The load factors (complexity and sophistication of each movement) are 38% in pre-effort and 45% in directional shape indicating a child of average intelligence.

Rhythms

When the effort-shape graphs were compared to that of the flow rhythms, affinities (oral-spacial effort, horizontal shape; anal-gravitational effort, vertical shape; urethral-temporal effort, sagittal shape) appear to be lopsided as well. There is a heavy loading of oral, oral sadistic, and feminine libidinal rhythms suggesting that Jim was still struggling with early maternal dependency. Aggressive behavior was thus expressed only at the oral level. He seemed to have acquired vertical movements via his identification with his mother rather than from related anal rhythms (as shown by the amount of feminine rhythms). This fixation was further demonstrated by the fact that 60 out of 76 mixed rhythms have either oral, feminine or both components. The sequential patterns of his rhythms showed Jim gradually working himself up to more masculine rhythms proceeded immediately by more feminine rhythms.

Summary

The adapted profile showed a dependent 5 year old who continually acted in a darting sudden manner without investment or

[1] Kestenberg, op. cit. Irmgard Bartenieff, "Effort Observation and Effort Assessment in Rehabilitation," Dance Notation Bureau Reprint, 1962. Kestenberg, "Psychology of Movement," Course at Dance Notation Bureau, New York.

forethought denoting a desire to, but fear of, aggressive behavior as well as manifesting a possible counterphobic reaction of rushing into danger.

Rx

1. Increase verbal awareness of motor behavior (Thought process)

2. Phallic rhythm (Flow rhythm)

3. Purification of rhythms (Flow rhythm)

4. Increase attention span (Effort/shape)

5. Broaden pre-effort profile particularly:

   gentle-sudden to intense-sudden and
   gentle-deliberate

6. Investment of aggressive drive in external objects (Drive-object)

7. Semi-autonomous relationship with therapist (with the placement of demands on the appropriateness of behavior) (Dyadic)

Treatment commenced with the formulation of an egocentric relationship with the therapist. The therapy sessions, for the most part, took the form of movement-drama interactions. Imaginary symbolic situations were utilized to work through more age appropriate expression of feelings as well as readapting a lopsided profile. The primary image chosen by Jim was that of a monster. The therapist was at first the object of the monster's oral aggressive behavior, but after a short period of time, the therapist was asked to become a "fellow monster" and "good mother" working with him to resolve some of his oedipal fears so that he was finally able to identify with a more masculine age-appropriate repertoire. During this process he was weaned away from mother monster as well as from his oral sadistic expression of anger to that of the utilization of phallic rhythms and the use of more intensity in his dynamics.

As the therapeutic process continued, he could maintain his attention on one fantasy for the full one hour session. There were periods of quiet with more deliberate movements as well as further needed clarification of rhythms.

Demands were placed on Jim in the way of suggestions for variations of his movement patterns, e.g., "Let's creep up on him (policeman, doctor, male monster) very slowly so he doesn't hear us and then pounce on him with all our might."[2] Jim's verbi-

---

[2] These male figures were father substitutes of Jim's used to resolve his oedipal strivings.

lization increased from one and two word responses to elaborate descriptions of fantasies. Much of the verbal integrative process was conducted via the therapist talking to an imaginary figure explaining to the figure why Jim could be mad and how in various situations he had a right to his feelings.

MRS. G.

Mrs. G. was a 72 year old widow who was referred to the movement therapist for treatment. She was seen individually by a psychotherapist as well as in a group in which the movement therapist was a co-leader. Mrs. G. was diagnosed as having a depressive reaction and as being in the initial stages of senility. It was decided that she be placed in a group after an initial period of individual sessions.

Mrs. G. was seen by the therapist in an initial evaluation session. Her fear regarding the loss of her memory was prominent. She asked where she was every few minutes and if someone knew where to pick her up. Her movements were stiff and tense, similar to a wooden soldier's. She was extremely fearful of falling which made her even more prone to do so. It was as if she had renounced the free flow of tension when using any of the complete effort-shape combinations. Even at the gestural level she was unable to experience these dynamics without tensing and going into bound flow.

Rx

1. Restore her movement repertoire (E/S, P-G)

2. Increase flow and relaxation (Flow of breath)

3. Provide for expression of feelings of fears and anger (Drive-object)

4. Egocentric group

Mrs. G. seemed to improve daily. An initial repetitive dance dyadic interaction was maintained by the therapist to reinforce her memory of the experience. The one-to-one also afforded an opportunity to center on the release of some of her feelings. Gradually she remembered and would look forward to the Dance Therapy sessions with great joy. As she entered the group experience, she began to encourage the other group members. And as the tensions were released from her body, her movement repertoire began to manifest itself again. She would lead the group into quick patterns changing into jumps and hops. Her fear of falling had disappeared and was replaced by an agility which was uncanny for a woman of her age and size.

(Mrs. G. was assigned to a mixed group of individuals with

similar backgrounds, ages and problems. Music which related to her youth was played to bring back and reinforce her previous movement repertoire as well as to cathect associations which would facilitate verbalization in her other therapies.)

Often, another active role of a movement-dance therapist is that of a specialist in evaluation non-verbal behavior. The following is an example of such a staff consult:

Family Movement Evaluation

Family worker

mother   father

patient   movement therapist

Normally an evaluation of this sort is carried out by viewing a videotapie or film which shows all the individuals involved fully at all times. If this is impossible, the therapist-notator generally sits behind a two-way mirror. Both these alternatives were impossible in this setting so that the notational data had to be curtailed. I have chosen this evaluation to demonstrate how much an observer could pick up from a 30 minute session.

(The client is a 25 year old male, diagnosed as a possible ambulatory schizophrenic.)

Fred's (client) body was characteristically in a bound rigid state. He exhibited only peripheral gestures in the forearms and legs; however these movements were, for the most part, devoid of any dynamics. His seated posture was hollowed and shortened. His general shaping seemed to correspond to that of his mother's. She, in turn, was giving negative non-verbal cues to Fred which were watched carefully by him. For example, when asked by the family worker how she felt about Fred, she hollowed and shortened her abdomen stroking it as if she were in pain. Fred acknowledged his mother's verbalizations by moving his leg toward her when she spoke. It was difficult to determine by his ambiguous position whether he was blocking her or taking her in. Initially Fred did not respond to his father at all (who attempted to take on his son's posturing but, in contrast to the son's even flow, moved constantly in urethral rhythms). However, after about 20 minutes (in which his father constantly verbalized positive responses concerning Fred), he began to take on the same rhythm pattern in the calf of his leg which was closest to his father, as well as moving it toward his father when he spoke.

Summary

Fred exhibited an immobilized torso throughout. No verbalization was made by him; his breath was shallow. When asked a question by the group worker he would go into a high intensity bound state. No flow adjustments were made except on a peripheral level. He seemed to be an extremely controlled, angry, fearful young man struggling with an identification with a negative mother.

Group Study

Since the group that will be discussed is not a typical Dance-Movement Therapy group, I feel it necessary to briefly outline what is felt to be a "classic format" for the dance therapist. The following is what has generally been utilized with hospitalized patients. Although effort-shape terminology has been used, this format is also followed by those therapists who do not employ these concepts to describe their sessions.

Classic Dance-Movement groups generally involve an initial warm-up period in which the therapist, having gotten everyone together in a circle, commences the session by leading the group into a flow pattern (movements with no dynamics or spacial attributes). The goals are to (1) relax the group, and to "start the flow going" i.e. circulation with attention drawn to the body; (2) to provide a common movement pattern for all—one which is primary and can be observed in even the most regressed individuals; and (3) to provide a "blank canvas" upon which the patients might begin painting an expression of themselves. If the group consists of severely disturbed individuals, the flow will be initiated distally (hands and/or feet) and will gradually be evolved to include the whole body (a more postural pattern).

The therapist then looks around the circle and starts picking up and duplicating dynamics and shape which the patients or clients start to superimpose. If, for example, an individual starts to use quickness and indirectness along with flow, the therapist will take on that pattern communicating to that member that she is with him. At this point the second phase of the therapy session begins.

The goals of the second phase are, (1) to pick up and enlarge upon patterns which manifest themselves in the patient's repertoire toward (a) externalized drives and (b) more postural merger; (2) to attempt to include experience in all possible effort-shape combinations; and (3) given the above two goals, to bring the group to various emotionally expressive peak experiences followed by an evolution into more neutral less charged movements.

Thus the therapist might evolve the above mentioned pattern of quickness and indirectness into use of a weight factor (strength or lightness). If none appears in the group the therapist might choose the more indulging of the two as in this case it is the initial full effort pattern to be introduced. Thus a flick is utilized (quick, indirect, light). From this if there is no observed change into an alternate dynamic by individual(s) in the group, the therapist might

181

gradually change the intention toward space to produce a dab (quick, direct, light), and then if possible into a punch (quick, direct, strong). Shaping is dealt with concomitantly as is experience with more postural as well as various gestural patterns.

After a period of time experiencing this full fighting effort the therapist will look to see if anyone in the group is changing any of the dynamics, shape, or body involvement. If so, she might then pick up on that pattern and evolve the group into another experience.

Within this second phase dyadic or small group interaction sometimes occurs depending on the level of the group. The circle may come together, spread apart, move into a line like a train moving about the room, or break up and come back together. Imagery and verbalization is also sometimes used.

The third phase often involves a period of diminishing work with externalizing of drives with the goals of (1) insuring return of individual control mechanisms, [3] and (2) drawing the individual into inner awareness of what has occurred both in terms of perceptual feedback—body awareness, cognitive realization, and integration of the emotional expression. This is often carried out via a rest period in which music is played of a more relaxing pensive nature. It has also been brought about via a toning down of the movement into a whisper—one which is brought about by use of more indulging efforts (light, slow, indirect) with gradual evolution into flow.

Analysis of Group

The group that will be discussed consists not of hospitalized individuals but rather of students and fellow mental health workers who were interested in learning more about themselves and in dealing with conflict areas through the use of Dance-Movement Therapy.

The first portion of the initial session was devoted to establishing the contract for the weekly 3-1/2 to 4 hour groups. Self-awareness, conflict processing and resolution, the development of a more adequate body-image and more adaptive movement repertoire, as well as experience in interacting and being aware of others on a non-verbal level were brought up. During this discussion it was established that each member would maintain his or her own responsibility for letting known his or her desires; and if the group agreed, to then work toward carrying them out. This was as simple as changing a record or as complex as wanting to work on a problem area with the assistance of the group. The amount and form of the fee was also a personal decision.

The dance-movement therapist's role was clearly stated. I was to be a facilitator—one who would respond to the needs of the

---

[3] Behavior which is quite appropriate and encouraged in a Dance-Movement session is often quite inappropriate in other settings.

group by showing or involving them in ways to satisfy or work through the particular need or problem area. I stressed the individual maintenance of responsibility for letting their needs be known as well as for joining in or not in various processes in which other group members were interested. If the group or individual asked to deal with a certain area and if that area required a more structural approach, then, if all agreed, it would be used. However, no structure would be imposed unless asked for by group members.

Agreements were also made that barring physical injury, destruction, and others trying to take over another's responsibility as to what or how he or she "should" work; the door was open. An implicit contract was also made that individual crises took priority over what was occurring at that moment.

The group then opted into moving, a record was chosen by one of the members and each person was given a self-decided period of time to move in his own way while others followed sharing the person's feeling with him—each taking time to be with and getting to know each other.

The initial subsequent sessions were all structureless. These entailed the individual's entering the wooden floored mirrored room and essentially waiting, till getting in touch with their body and their wants, they felt like moving. One or two members might choose a record and start dancing. Another might join with them while another might wish to be on his own. Still another might stay seated for awhile near the door sensing his or her own timing for involvement. For some, it was a new experience to gradually become aware of where, what, when, how and with whom did one really want to move. Without pressure or demands, people began moving in ways they had either forgotten or had never experienced before.

As the group became more comfortable with their own movement needs and experimentation, individuals who had been "loners" started interacting with others in dyads and small groups. Many sessions were followed by a period of discussion in which sharing and feedback occurred.

During this period the therapist's role was that of a supporter. I would spend time moving with each individual, I danced with them in synchrony letting them know that I could be with them, that we could be together. With some the communication would evolve into reciprocal diagonal jabs at each other or mutual shoulder pushing. At other times communication would take the form of a rocking pattern while maintaining eye-to-eye contact for minutes at a time.

When individuals seem to want a group experience, e.g., triads drawing together; I would attempt to gently draw others who seemed willing into the interaction. This sometimes meant widening the circle, holding out an arm, incorporating someone into the elastic stretch rope, or gradually evolving an individual into the movement pattern of the group.

183

My role also consisted of being aware of when it was beneficial to "be" with a member and when it was important to allow someone to be by themselves during periods of discovery.

Although the members of the group had well functioning control mechanisms and ego systems, the eye "in the back of my head" was always open. On occasion, experience in novel situations—situations in which there has been minimal experience in the utilization of controls, can produce new and sometimes frightening sensations in an individual.

After this initial foundation of familiarity and trust had been established, the group began to ask for structure which would further help facilitate growth. Concurrently, individuals and dyads began verbally asking the group if they could "work." At these times, I would suggest various techniques to be utilized depending on the needs and problems. Gestalt, bioenergetic, effort/shape and psycho-motor methods were often used. Situations were restaged using members of the group who were "beaten up" with slashes and kicks. Other members observed this process and identified with the protagonist hero. On another occasion part of the group pinned an individual to the floor to help him to externalize the negative aspect of a conflict area and to personify more adaptive modes of behavior in a motorized exaggerated working out of being buried. At other times the whole group became involved in doing a certain exercise of which an individual was in particular need.

In this phase, the therapist's role was more directive, but I always reminded the individuals that I could not "make something happen." I could only suggest a way and guide them through the process. The rest was up to them. I stressed also sensing their own "right time" to move, keeping watch that the group's incentive did not over-ride the individual's. My role was also that of caretaker, making sure that no one left the sessions in a disorganized or defenseless state. Each member knew that I would be there to talk and/or work with them until they felt comfortable enough to depart. [4]

Thus if the reader recalls the Primary Group Levels of Organization, he or she will find this group progressing from a one-to-one parallel level, to a task level to that of an egocentric group cooperative level in which fellow members attended to each other's needs and responded by taking on various roles to help facilitate another's working through of an area of concern.

---

[4] When the set time is over in many groups (or individual sessions for that matter), many therapists will usher their client(s) out the door even if the individual is in the middle of a process. This is considered acceptable procedure of many. My own personal feeling is that the imposition of such a time superstructure often detracts from the therapeutic process as well as the relationship. The contract of "I will listen or be with you for one hour, but at the end of that time my ear and self is dead to you till next week," is in my opinion, bizarre when the person is essentially being asked to respond and interact in a "spontaneous" manner.

BATTLE FOR SPRING: AN INITIAL SESSION

I have often been asked by my students "How do you begin with a client? What do you do? What do you say?" These questions seem to be of particular importance when in private practice where the referral to dance/movement therapy may be as general as "I think this individual could benefit from work with you." Here there is usually no chart, no nurses to consult, and no access, prior to the session to observe and possibly notate the individual's movement sequences to ascertain a profile.

Such was the case with Helen, who phoned one afternoon to make an appointment. With adequately functioning adults, people who seek help because, as Dr. Bernstein puts it, "you don't have to be sick to want to feel better," I feel in many instances that I have an ally against dysfunction. We exist within a partnership and share in the responsibility for the goals and the process of working toward them. Therefore, my "colleague" and I crystallize the maladapture behavior, evolve the contract; and select the method of therapeutic adaptive activities together. Utilizing strong eclectism in approaches under one frame of reference avails the client several alternative routes to awareness and function.

Initial Therapy Session:

We sat together for the first portion of the session and I asked her what brought her here, and what she felt she would like to work on. Helen, an overweight, sluggish woman in her 40's, shared with me, "My back has been aching and I've realized that putting on Ben-Gay is not going to help."

I suggested that the sustained removal of her backache be at least an initial goal in therapy and that we could work from there. She agreed. I then suggested several ways to work, thus affording her part of the responsibility of selecting the method, dance, classid Gestalt, breath release neo-Reichian patterns, body correctives, and massage were the avenues offered. She selected one of the more passive methods: massage.

Helen lay on her stomach and I began massaging her back, pressing and releasing with the flow of her breath. The painful area was easily found both visually and by touch. The muscles of her scapula girdle were bound and cold to the touch. Her breathing was excluded from this area as well.

"If your upper back pain could talk, what would it say, Helen?", I asked. "I keep her down. . .Keep her from experiencing spring. . .from being happy and from getting in touch with her own strength." She then made an allusion to a part of Solomon's "The Song of Songs" in the Bible. A metaphor to spring, "The season of glad songs has come, the cooing of the turtledove is heard in our land."

I noticed that her feet were becoming more bound as she tensely intertwined them with wrings (strong, sustained, indirect movement). I touched them; they were extremely cold from the lack of circulation.

As I rubbed them, she spoke, "I am Helen's feet. I'm afraid. I'm afraid. I tense up every time she tries to stand on me. My toes curl up. I won't let her stand on her own two feet. She'll have to depend on other support."

I suggested that she stand; and as she did, the tension rose up her legs.

"Walk around and allow whatever feeling with its voice to evolve." Her step became stronger, quicker, and more direct. I encouraged her to stamp; and as she did the voice of her foot tension could be heard, "I won't budge! I won't budge!"

I noticed that her arms lacked the strength of operation. Her shoulders were cutting off their power producing a flailing pattern. Moving with her in synchrony I assisted her into a posture-gesture merger of the punch lower torso pattern having the flow of her breath coordinate and initiate the movement from the center of weight.

Helen was still internally conflicted; part of her wanted to move, to stand on her own two feet, to be independent while the other part wanted her to remain dependent and helpless within the gestalt. I attempted to externalize the defense by becoming that part of her who wanted her to remain blocked.

"Don't move! You won't move!" I yelled in a P-G merging pattern. "I will move!" she retorted in a similar pattern. We continued till it seemed Helen had felt this side of her assert itself throughout her whole body.

After having her stand in a now more centered stance sensing the vibrations of her re-claimed body, she relaxed supine on a foam mat. From this position the throbbing of her jaw and neck could easily be seen. Both had an extreme bound flow utilized in order to block her feelings from conscious recognition and expression. Helen still felt the conflict battling in her jaw: a desire to express aggression orally (perhaps in its primitive form to bite out and snap at someone), with a counteracting attempt to hold that expression back.

I suggested the bio-energetic technique of biting and holding a towel with her teeth and jaw. This seemed to protract and release some of the tension such that I felt she could begin to express and release this localized, repressed affect. We began moving in synchrony on all fours glaring and snapping at each other like lionesses. She was encouraged to breathe deep into her pelvic girdle and allow growls to emerge.

186

As the activity seemed to come to a natural termination I suggested to Helen to find a place in this room and a body position that seemed comfortable to her and to then allow herself to draw her attention inward. I asked her to move her awareness throughout her body and to seek out part or parts which she felt less than others, which may be numb, colder, more tense, or tingle. These areas are often "cloudier" in terms of readily available visual fantasies. However, I asked her to try to see if any images came to mind when centering on the identified areas.

After several minutes, Helen shared with me that she had an image of a tight umbilical cord wrapped around her cervix. She said that she was keeping her children tied to her with this cord, as well as having it tie off her unreleased anger and sadness at being unable to allow herself to experience her own spring—her re-birth.

I said that she looked sad. And slowly, tears began to appear. After a while I mentioned that sadness often comes from feelings of loss. She then spoke of the process of losing her old identity and of evolving toward a new one. It seemed to me that there were two conflicted parts in Helen, one which wants to keep her in a static identity in "winter" as she symbolized it with all the cold anger, sadness, and fear locked inside—the part that keeps her umbilical cord and bound tension in her body; and the other part which seems to be getting tired of the pain—the part that brought her to seek help—the part that wants her to grow to be re-born.

I suggested that perhaps the contract could be expanded to include the resolution of these two aspects within the gestalt so that her body would not have to continue to be a battleground for the assaults and counter-attacks of these polarities.

In a sense, this was Helen's fight for her "spring" for her Easter, as she put it. "It has been 42 years," she said, "Long enough."

With this contract in mind, subsequent sessions entailed a searching for the etiology or inception of the point at which dysfunction took priority over growth. The movement therapy sessions became a series of microcosms in which to try out more adaptive behavior to be integrated into her total environment.

CHAPTER IX

Conclusion

Now, after you have read through this outline, digest what makes sense to you—what feels right—and disgard the rest. Each therapist is going to work just a little bit differently then the guy next to him—a highly favorable situation I might add. What we don't need in this or any other field are a group of programmed robots moving and responding in identical, totally predetermined patterns.

This book is meant to give the reader a taste of how one person sees the relationship between one philosophical approach and one modality. All of what has been written here "feels right to me." I have, however, seen it work enough times to feel it worthwhile to pass it on to you. My hope is that this book becomes one of many resource books which are used when brain storming is needed. It is not meant to be a blinder to your own or anyone else's creative process. The suggested movement activities are only examples from a myriad of experiences which could be used. By combining your thoughts with some of the ideas expressed here, creativity can be exercised not suppressed.

Neither is this book meant to stiffle spontaniety and "here and now" reactions to "here and now" situations. Going into a therapy session with your head filled with specific exercises, goals, etc. is, in my opinion, one of the worst possible mistakes a therapist can make. This situation only serves to desensitize the person to where the client is and how he feels at that moment. I do not mean to suggest either that a therapist be totally unaware of the direction they both feel they should work toward. However, there is an optimim compromise: one in which the therapist reacts to the "here and now": of where his client or clients are such that he could be able to duplicate the mood tone from his own feelings if need be in order to sense the people with whom he is working. The "treatment plan," then, is placed in reserve or subliminal awareness if you will—far enough away so that it only comes to the forefront when needed.

Ideally, however, there would be no necessity for even an occasional calling forth of such data. If this information is truly integrated, it will flow within the breath pulse of the movement therapist in spontaneous client-centered movement interactions.

189

Appendix

Developmental Chart

Gesell, Piaget, and Effort-Shape Developmental Correlation

Levels of Organization Form for Dance-Movement Therapy

Maladaptive Behavior Evaluation Form

CONSTELLATIONS	0-1 mons.	1-6 mons.	6 mons.-1 yr.	1-1½ yrs.	1½-2 yrs.	2-3 yrs.	3-4 yrs.
Flow of Breath	Normal Breath Flow						
Effort	Primal Regulation of Tension Flow		Spacial Pre-effort	Gravitational Pre-effort		Time Pre-effort	
Shape	Symmetrical and Asymmetrical Shape Flow		Horizontal Dimensional Shape	Vertical Dimensional Shape		Sagittal Dimensional Shape	
Posture-Gesture	P-G Flow						
Flow Rhythms	Oral Libidinal		Oral Aggressive	Anal Libidinal	Anal Sadistic	Urethral Libidinal	Urethral Sadistic
Body-Image		Positive Affect in Self	Body, Body Part Relationship / Body Differentiate from Environment		Movement of the Body Through Space		
Drive-Object		Libidinal Self Investment	External Libidinal Investment	Investment in Aggressive Drive in External Object			
Dyadic		Ego-Centric	Object-Dependent		Object-Ambivalent	Semi-Autonomous	
GROUP	One-to-One					Parallel	Task
RITES OF PASSAGE	Birth Ritual Process		Weaning Ritual Process				
TACTILE PERCEPTION		Recognition	Discriminate		Recall		
KINESTHETIC PERCEPTION		Recognition	Discriminate		Recall		
VESTIBULAR PERCEPTION		Recognition	Discriminate		Recall		
COGNITIVE REPRESENTATION		Enactive				Iconic	
THOUGHT PROCESS	Primary Process					Secondary Process	
PLAY-WORK							

4-5	5-6	6-7	7-8	8-9	9-10	10-11	11-12	12-15	15-18	18-20		65-
Space Effort	Weight Effort	Temporal Effort		2 Effort Combination				3 Effort Combination				
Horizontal Shaping	Vertical Shaping	Sagittal Shaping		2 Shape Combination				3 Shape Combination				
Effort-Shape Gesture Mergers								E-S P-G Mergers				
Feminine Libidinal Aggressive	Phallic Libidinal Aggressive						Phallic-Feminine					
	Sexual Identity											
			Chumship					Autonomous				
	Ego-Centric Cooperative											
						Puberty Ritual Process			Marriage Ritual Process			Retirement Ritual Process
Iconic							Abstract					
Secondary Process								Tertiary Process				
					Dance as Hobby			Dance as Occupation				

193

Age	Effort	Shape
0-1 mon.	Primal regulation of tension flow	Symmetrical and asymmetrical shape flow
1-6 mon.	Ability to initiate, continue, and cessate free and bound flow interchanges.	Alternation of bipolar growing and shrinking and ability to shape in a unipolar relationship to the environment.
6-9 mon.	Spacial pre-effort	Horizontal dimensional shape
	Ability to channel and be flexible	Ability to shape sideways and across the body
9-12 mon.		Communication
1-1 1/2	Gravitational or weight pre-effort	Vertical dimensional shape
	Ability to move with vehemence and gentility	Ability to shape upwards and downwards
		Presentation
1 1/2-2		
	Time pre-effort	Sagittal dimensional shape
2-3	Ability to move with suddenness and hesitation	Ability to shape forwards and backwards
3-4		Operation

Piaget	Gesell

Sensori-motor: Reflex stage
    Hereditary organic reflexes
    Sucking and grasping
	Grasp reflex
	Sucking reflex

Sensori-motor: Primary circular reactions
    First acquired adaptations
    Concepts of groups and reversibility without mental representation
    Voluntary movements
	Grasp reflex lost; raises head
	Initiates arm in grasping object
	Clutches

Sensori-motor: Secondary circular reactions
    Movement centered on maintaining results produced in environment
    Intentional adaptations
    Foresight and incipient goal directed behavior
	Assumes crawling posture
	Creeps
	Transfers object from hand to hand

Sensori-motor: Coordination of secondary schema
    Emergence of means end relationship
    Beginning of sign understanding
    Concept of object permanence
	Site
	Brings two objects together

Sensori-motor: Tertiary circular reactions
    Stabilization of object permanence
    Discovery of new means through active experimentation
	Cruses with support
	Crude release
	Pincer grasp

Sensori-motor: Inventions of new means through mental combinations
    Internalization of sensori-motor schema
    Use of foresight in solving sensori-motor problems
	Walks without support
	Fine manipulative skill

Pre-operational II: Pre-conceptual substage
    Extracting concepts from sensory experiences
    Language—verbal communication
    Presentation and representation of objects
	Runs
	Regards and reaches simultaneously

Transduction—reasoning from particular to particular without generalization
    Syncretism—linking of unrelated material
    Realism—illegitimate generalization
    Artificialism—belief that natural events are caused by humans
	Up and down stairs
	Jumps down 12 inches
	Stands on one foot

Egocentrism in language and thought	Runs smoothly at different speeds Alternates progression in climbing

Age	Effort	Shape
4-5	**Spacial effort** Ability to move with directness and indirectness	**Horizontal shaping** Ability to shape in the horizontal plane with spreading and enclosing movements
5-6	**Gravitational or weight effort** Ability to move with strength and lightness	**Vertical shaping** Ability to shape in the vertical plane with ascending and descending movements
6-7	**Time efforts** Ability to move with acceleration or quickness and deceleration or slowness	**Sagittal shaping** Ability to shape in the sagittal plane with advancing and retreating movements
8-12	**Inner attitudes—2 effort combinations** Movement involving temporal-spacial, spacial-gravitational, and temporal-gravitational factors	**2 Shaping combinations** Movement involving horizontal-vertical, horizontal-sagittal, and vertical-sagittal shaping factors
12-15	**Full efforts—3 effort combinations** Ability to float, glide, dab, flick, press, wring, slash, punch	**3 Shaping combinations** Movement involving attributes from each of the three planes: horizontal, sagittal, and vertical

Piaget	Gesell

Pre-operational II: Intuitive Substage
   Manipulation of experimental objects more effectively
   Cannot yet consider two or more dimensions at the same time, but focuses on one aspect at a time
	Long swinging steps
	Stops and goes quickly
	Throws overhead

	Walks on toes Climbs and skips Narrow symmetrical controlled motions Grasping coordination
	Constant activity Approaches activity with more abandon and/or deliberation Interest in stunts and tools

Concrete Operations
   Operational stage in logical thinking
   Groupings of operations using: conservation, associativity, identity, reversibility, substitution, multiplication of classes and series, and tree of classes
   Emergence of grouping of combinations
	Repeat skills to master
	Timing under better control
	Competitive sports
	Handwriting a tool

Formal Operations
   Combination of operations and schema
   Abstract thought
   Ability to deal with a wide variety of complex relations (e.g., ability to move using all possible combinations of effort-shape attributes)
   Formulation of assumptions and hypotheses
   Reflective thinking
   Concepts of continuity, infinity, symbolism
	Learns hobby and job skills
	Copes with environment using gross and fine motor skills

NAME:_____ AGE:____DATE:_____

Diagnosis:

Conflicting Physical Disability:

Characteristic Movement Profile and Summary:

Rx:

LEVELS OF ORGANIZATION FORM FOR DANCE-MOVEMENT THERAPY

PENNY BERNSTEIN, MA, OTR, DTR

Flow of Breath

    1. Breath flow

    2. Breathing in the service of movement

Effort Levels of Organization

    1. Primal regulation of tension flow

    2. Spatial pre-effort

    3. Gravitational pre-effort

    4. Temporal pre-effort

    5. Spatial effort

    6. Gravitational effort

    7. Temporal effort

    8. Inner attitudes—(2-effort combination)

    9. Full efforts—(3-effort combination)

Shape Levels of Organization

    1. Symmetrical shape flow

    2. Asymmetrical shape flow

    3. Horizontal directional shape

    4. Vertical directional shape

    5. Sagittal directional shape

    6. Horizontal shaping

    7. Vertical shaping

    8. Sagittal shaping

    9. 2-shape combination

    10. 3-shape combination

Posture-Gesture Levels of Organization

    1. Posture-gesture flow

    2. Merging of gesture systems

    3. Merging of posture-gesture systems

Tension Flow Rhythms Levels of Organization

1. Oral libidinal	
2. Oral aggressive	
3. Anal libidinal	
4. Anal sadistic	
5. Urethral libidinal	
6. Urethral sadistic	
7. Inner genital libidinal	
8. Inner genital sadistic	
9. Phallic libidinal	
10. Phallic sadistic	
11. Phallic-inner genital (genital adult)	

Body-Image Levels of Organization

1. Investment of positive affect in body	
2. Differentiation of body from the environment	
3. Recognition of the body parts and their relationship	
4. Movement of the body through space	
5. Sexual identity	

Drive-Object Levels of Organization

1. Investment of libidinal drive in self	
2. Investment of libidinal drive in external objects	
3. Investment of aggressive drive in external objects	

Dyadic Levels of Organization

1. Egocentric	
2. Object-dependent	
3. Object-ambivalent	
4. Semi-autonomous	
5. Chumship	
6. Autonomous	

Group Levels of Organization

    1. One-to-one

    2. Parallel

    3. Task

    4. Ego-centric and group cooperative

Rites of Passage Levels of Organization

    1. Birth Ritual Process

    2. Weaning Ritual Process

    3. Puberty Ritual Process

    4. Marriage Ritual Process

    5. Retirement Ritual Process

Tactile Perceptual Levels of Organization

    1. Tactile recognition

    2. Tactile discrimination

    3. Tactile retention and recall

Kinesthetic Perceptual Levels of Organization

    1. Kinesthetic recognition

    2. Kinesthetic discrimination

    3. Kinesthetic retention and recall

Vestibular Perceptual Levels of Organization

    1. Vestibular recognition

    2. Vestibular discrimination

    3. Vestibular retention and recall

Cognitive Representation Levels of Organization

    1. Enactive

    2. Iconic

    3. Abstract

Thought Processes Levels of Organization

1. Primary process
2. Secondary process
3. Tertiary process

Play-Work Levels of Organization

1. Dance as a hobby
2. Dance as an occupation

MALADAPTIVE BEHAVIOR
DANCE-MOVEMENT THERAPY EVALUATION FORM

PENNY BERNSTEIN MA, OTR, DTR

Flow of Breath

1. Breathing shallow and below normal	
2. Hypernea	
3. Air sucked in	
4. Vertical breath pattern	
5. Breath held	
6. Decreased breath rate	
7. Immobilization of chest	
8. Immobilization of diaphragm	
9. Immobilization of pelvis	
10. Immobilization of abdomen	
11. Flaccid-limp	
12. Body or body part muscular rigidity, "dead spots"	
13. Mute	
14. Shallow vocalization	
15. Rapid speech	
16. Slow speech	

Effort Levels of Organization

1. Inability to distinguish movement continuity/discontinuity	
2. Lack of an adaptive range of tension flow variations	
3. Dominance or excessive bound flow	
4. Dominance or excessive free flow	
5. Dominance of neutral flow	
6. Difficulty in adaptive usage of channeling	
7. Difficulty in adaptive usage of flexibility	
8. Difficulty in adaptive usage of vehemence	

9. Difficulty in adaptive usage of gentleness	
10. Difficulty in adaptive usage of hesitation	
11. Difficulty in adaptive usage of suddenness	
12. Difficulty in adaptive usage of directness	
13. Difficulty in adaptive usage of indirectness	
14. Lack of adequate ability to investigate or define	
15. Difficulty in adaptive usage of lightness	
16. Difficulty in adaptive usage of strength	
17. Lack of adequate ability to utilize determination, persistence, conviction, and/or firmness or purpose	
18. Difficulty in adaptive usage of slowness	
19. Difficulty in adaptive usage of quickness	
20. Lack of an adequate sense of timing or decisiveness	
21. Difficulty in adaptive use of a two effort quality	
22. Unadaptive exaggeration of an inner attitude	
23. Difficulty in adaptively utilizing a 3-effort combination	

Shape Levels of Organization

1. Difficulty in adaptive usage of symmetrical shape flow	
2. Excessive bound bulging: feelings of bursting with anger	
3. Excessive bound lengthening: rage and/or anxiety state	
4. Excessive bound widening: fear of falling apart	
5. Excessive bound hollowing: feelings of being knotted up	
6. Excessive bound shortening: feelings of being wound up	

7. Excessive bound narrowing: feelings of emptiness	
8. Predominance of hollowing, shortening, and/or narrowing	
9. Predominance of bulging, lengthening, and/or widening	
10. Difficulty in relating to the inner space of the body	
11. Bizarre, manneristic shaping	
12. Difficulty in adaptive usage of asymmetrical shape flow	
13. A continuous maladaptive asymmetrical body stance	
14. Lack of reaction to a descrete stimulus	
15. Inappropriate movement response to a positive and/or negative stimulus	
16. Difficulty in adaptive usage of sideways direction	
17. Difficulty in adaptive usage of movement across the body	
18. Difficulty in adaptive usage of upwards direction	
19. Difficulty in adaptive usage of downwards direction	
20. Difficulty in adaptive usage of forward direction	
21. Difficulty in adaptive usage of backward direction	
22. Difficulty with adaptive use of spreading	
23. Difficulty in adaptive usage of enclosing	
24. Lack of an adequate awareness of the range of possibilities or the ability to explore	
25. Difficulty in adaptive usage of ascending	
26. Difficulty in adaptive usage of descending	
27. Lack of an adequate ability to confront	
28. Difficulty in adaptive usage of advancing	
29. Difficulty in adaptive usage of retreating	
30. Lack of an adequate sense of anticipation, farsightedness and sense of the effects of the present in relation to the future	
31. Difficulty in adaptive usage of 2-shape combinations	
32. Difficulty in adaptive usage of 3-shape combinations	

Effort-Shape Relationship

    1. Difficulty in appropriate effort-shape combination

    2. Lopsided effort-shape affinities within movement repertoire

Posture-Gesture Levels of Organization

    1. Difficulty in adaptive flow variation in postures

    2. Difficulty in E-S flow P-G mergers

    3. Difficulty in adaptive E-S G mergers

    4. Difficulty in E-S G-P or P-G mergers

    5. Gestures unrelated to postures (or vice-versa)

    6. Artificial movements (diminished postural adjustments)

    7. Doll-like or puppet-like movements

    8. Idiosyncratic bizarre movements as compensation for inability to merge

    9. Predominance of inadaptive peripheral gestures

    10. Lack of adaptibility of postures

    11. Lack of posturally expressed affect

Tension Flow Rhythm Levels of Organization

    1. Insufficient amount of oral rhythms

    2. Excessive amount of oral rhythms

    3. Continuous and/or diffuse crying

    4. Vomiting or nausea

    5. Tense deep neck muscles; upper back

    6. Back arched, stiffening, resistance of arm and leg extension

    7. Insufficient amount of oral aggressive rhythms

    8. Excessive amount of oral aggressive rhythms

    9. Tense throat, jaw, chest, eyes

    10. Restless grasping

    11. Blowing, spitting, biting

    12. Insufficient amount of anal rhythms

    13. Excessive amount of anal rhythms

14. Continuous kicking and slapping	
15. Insufficient amount of anal sadistic rhythms	
16. Excessive amounts of anal sadistic rhythms	
17. Retroflexed anal sadistic rhythms	
18. Tense buttocks, thighs, calves and shoulders	
19. Pelvis tilted forward; upward	
20. Insufficient amount of urethral rhythms	
21. Excessive amount of urethral rhythms	
22. Insufficient amount of urethral sadistic rhythms	
23. Flowing everywhere with little control	
24. Excessive amounts of urethral sadistic rhythms	
25. Tense lower pelvis	
26. Insufficient amount of feminine rhythms	
27. Excessive amounts of feminine rhythms	
28. Insufficient amounts of feminine sadistic rhythms	
29. Excessive amounts of feminine sadistic rhythms	
30. Insufficient amounts of phallic rhythms	
31. Excessive amounts of phallic rhythms	
32. Insufficient amounts of phallic sadistic rhythms	
33. Excessive amounts of phallic sadistic rhythms	
34. Inappropriate oediple resolution	
35. Insufficient amounts of adult genital rhythms	
36. Excessive mixture of o, a, or u rhythms with others	
37. Lack of presence of phase appropriate pure rhythms	

Body-Image Levels of Organization

1. Negative B-I	
2. Unkempt clothes, poor hygenic care	
3. Self mutilation, suicidal ideation	
4. Difficulty in adaptively differentiating the body from the environment	

5. Body boundaries lack adaptive bound flow and shrinking in shape flow

6. Fear of dismemberment

7. Difficulty in recognizing body parts

8. Difficulty in identifying body parts

9. Difficulty in recognizing body part relationship

10. Difficulty in differentiating internal from external

11. B-I distortions: size, shape, absence, presence

12. Difficulty in moving through space

13. Difficulty in adaptive motor planning

14. Laterality dominance and/or inadequate reciprocal movement

15. Insufficient amount of genital rhythms

16. Bound pelvis

Drive-Object Levels of Organization

1. Inappropriate inhibition of libidinal rhythms

2. Insufficient amount of indulging pre-efforts

3. Difficulty in the adaptive use of indulging efforts and corresponding shape

4. Difficulty in adaptive use of fighting efforts, pre-efforts and corresponding shape

5. Lack of postural merger of aggression

6. Denial of anger

7. Fear of letting go

8. Diffuse, non-directed anger, i.e., no use of space

9. Difficulty in the use of strength when expressing anger

10. Difficulty in the use of quickness when expressing anger

11. Lack of aggressive movements when confronted with an aggressive object

Dyadic Levels of Organization

1. Inability in merging movement pattern with therapist

2. Difficulty in formulating a trust relationship

210

3. Difficulty in differentiating from primary object	
4. Difficulty in self-initiating or cessating movement	
5. Inappropriate negative response to authority figure	
6. Over-dependent relationship with therapist	
7. Inability to satisfy the needs of another	

Group Levels of Organization

1. Inability to engage in D-MT in the presence of others	
2. Difficulty in sharing a movement session with others	
3. Preoccupation with competition	
4. Difficulty in involving self in short term tasks	
5. Difficulty in adopting group roles	
6. Exhibitionistic	
7. Wants to dominate the group	
8. Refuses to lead the group	
9. Lack of minimal tolerance for closeness	
10. Fear of dissolution of identity in a group	

Rites of Passage Levels of Organization

1. Repressed fear from the birth trauma	
2. Lack of basic trust in dyadic movement interactions	
3. Difficulty in initiating any movement activities	
4. Love-hate ambivalence with individuals of the opposite sex	
5. Lack of sense of identity	
6. Child-like or immature movement repertoire	
7. Difficulty in commitment (vertical shape)	
8. Sense of despair (flaccid, limp)	
9. Sense of alienation and separateness (hollow and narrow and shortened shap flow)	

Tactile Perceptual Levels of Organization

1. Excess amount of free flow	
2. Lack of adaptive response to tactile stimulation	
3. Tactile defensivenss	

4. Seeks touch, clings

5. Difficulty in differentiating tactile stimulation

6. Difficulty in discriminating between positive and negative stimulation

7. Difficulty in retaining and recalling tactile stimulation

Kinesthetic Perceptual Levels of Organization

1. Difficulty in recognizing proprioceptive stimuli

2. Difficulty in recognizing vibratory stimuli

3. Difficulty in discriminating or localizing kinesthetic stimuli

4. Poor position sense

5. Difficulty in retaining and recalling kinesthetic stimuli

Vestibular Perceptual Levels of Organization

1. Difficulty in sensing or reacting to vestibular stimuli

2. Continuous loss of balance

3. Difficulty in discriminating vibratory stimuli

4. Difficulty in retaining and recalling stimuli and/or the appropriate response

Cognitive Representation Levels of Organization

1. Difficulty in enactive cognition

2. Difficulty in iconic cognition

3. Difficulty in abstract cognition

Thought Process Levels of Organization

1. Predominance of primary process thought	
2. Dominance of symbolic inadaptive ritualized movement	
3. Inability to differentiate between primary and secondary process thought	

Play-Work Levels of Organization

1. Body insufficiently conditioned	
2. Difficulty in moving improvisationally	
3. Difficulty in creative problem solving	

Bibliography

Books

Allport, J.W. and Vernon, P.E. Studies in Expressive Movement. New York: The Macmillan Company, 1933.

Arnheim, Rudolf. Toward a Psychology of Art. Los Angeles: University of California Press, 1966.

Bartenieff, Irmagard and Davis, Martha Ann. Effort-Shape Analysis of Movement: The Unity of Expression and Function. Bronx, New York: Albert Einstein College of Medicine, 1963.

Beard, Ruth. An Outline of Piaget's Developmental Psychology for Students and Teachers. New York: Basic Books, Inc., 1969.

Birdwhistle, Ray. Introduction to Kinesics. Microfilm-Xerography. Louisville, Michigan: University of Louisville, 1967. (Also in FSC.)

_____. Kinesics and Context. Philadelphia: University of Pennsylvania, 1970.

Butter, Charles. Neuropsychology: The Study of Brain and Behavior. Belmont, Brooks/Cole Publishing Co., 1968.

Christiansen, Bjorn. Thus Speaks the Body. New York: Anno Press, 1972.

Cumming, John and Cumming, Elaine. Ego and Milieu. New York: Atherlon Press, 1966.

Dell, Cecily. A Primer for Movement Description. Dance Notation Bureau, 1970.

Doubler, Margaret H. Dance: A Creative Art Experience. Madison: The University of Wisconsin Press, 1968.

Dunbar, Flanders. Emotions and Bodily Changes. New York: Columbia University Press, 1954.

Erikson, Erik. Childhood and Society. New York: W.W. Norton and Co., 1963.

Evan, Blanche. The Child's World: Its Relation to Dance Pedagogy. New York: Dance Therapy Center, 1948.

Fast, Julius. Body Language. New York: M. Evans & Co., 1970.

Federn, Paul. Ego Psychology and the Psychosis. New York: Basic Books, Inc., 1952.

Feldman, Sandor, M.D. Mannerisms of Speech and Gestures. New York: International Universities Press, 1971.

Fiorentino, Mary. Reflex Testing for Evaluating C.N.S. Development. Springfield: Charles C. Thomas, 1965.

Ford, Donald and Urban, Hugh. Systems of Psychotherapy.
New York: John Wiley and Sons, Inc., 1967.

Freud, Anna. Normality and Pathology in Childhood. New York:
International Universities Press, 1966.

Freud, Anna. The Psychoanalytic Treatment of Children.
New York: Schocken Books, 1966.

Freud, Sigmund. An Outline of Psychoanalysis. New York:
W. W. Norton & Co., 1949.

Gaston, E. Mayer, Ph. D. Music in Therapy. New York:
Macmillar Company, 1968.

Gordon, Jesse. (Ed.) Handbook of Clinical and Experimental
Hypnosis. New York: Macmillan Company, 1967.

Gunther, Bernard. Sense Relaxation Below Your Mind. New York:
Macmillan Company, 1968.

Hartman, Heinz. Ego Psychology and the Problem of Adaptation.
New York: International Universities Press, 1958.

Jung, Carl. Man and His Symbols. New York: Doubleday &
Company, 1964.

_____. The Practice of Psychotherapy. New York: Pantheon
Books, 1954.

Kephart, Newell. The Slow Learner in the Classroom. Columbus,
Ohio: Charles Merrill Books, 1960.

King, Bruce. Creative Dance Experience for Learning. New York:
Bruck King Studio, 1968.

Kubie, Lawrence. Neurotic Distortion of the Creative Process.
Kansas: University of Kansas Press, 1968.

Kris, Ernst. Psychoanalytic Explorations in Art. New York:
Schocken Books, 1967.

Laban, Rudolf and Lawrence, F. C. Effort. London: MacDonald
and Evans, 1947.

Laban, Rudolf. The Mastery of Movement. London: MacDonald
and Evans, 1960.

Lamb, Warren and Turner, David. Management Behavior.
New York: International Universities Press, 1969.

_____. Posture and Gesture. London: Gerald Duckworth
& Co., Ltd., 1965.

Langer, Jonas; Mussen, Paul; and Covington, Martin. (Eds.)
Trends and Issues in Developmental Psychology. New York:
Holt, Rinehart & Winston, 1969.

Langer, Jonas. Theories of Development. New York: Holt,
Rinehart and Winston, 1969.

Lifton, Walter. Working With Groups. New York: John Wiley
and Sons, 1966.

Lomax, Alan. Folk Song Style and Culture. Washington, D.C.:
Plimpton Press, 1968.

Lowen, Alexander. The Betrayal of the Body. New York:
Macmillan Company, 1967.

_____. The Language of the Body. New York: Collier Books,
1971.

Machover, Karen. Personality Projection in the Drawing of the
Human Figure. Springfield: Charles C. Thomas, 1949.

Manual on Administration. New York: American Occupational
Therapy Assoc., 1965.

McGraw, Myrtle. The Neuromuscular Maturation of the Human
Infant. New York: Hafner Company, 1966.

Meerloo, Joost A.M. Creativity and Eternization: Essays on
Creative Instinct. New York: Humanities Press, 1968.

Middleman, Ruth. The Non-Verbal Method in Working with Groups.
New York: Association Press, 1968.

Mosey, Anne. Occupational Therapy: Theory and Practice.
Medford: Pothier Bros., 1968.

Muss, Rolf. Theories of Adolescence. New York: Random House,
1969.

Mussen, Henry; Conger, John; and Kagan, Jerome. Child Development and Personality. New York: Harper and Row, 1963.

North, Marian. Personality Assessment Through Movement.
London: MacDonald and Evans, 1972.

Noyes, Arthur and Kolb, Lawrence. Modern Clinical Psychiatry.
Philadelphia: W.B. Saunders Company, 1964.

Pesso, Albert. Experience in Action. New York: New York University Press, 1973.

Piaget, Jean; Inhelder, Barbel; and Szeminska, Alina. The Child's
Conception of Geometry. New York: Basic Books, Inc.

_____. The Origins of Intelligence in Children. New York:
W.W. Norton & Co., 1963.

Perls, Frederick, M.D., Ph.D.; Hefferline, Ralph, Ph.D.;
Goodman, Paul, Ph.D. Gestalt Therapy. New York: Dell
Publishing Company, 1951.

Preston, Valerie. A Handbook for Modern Educational Dance. London: MacDonald & Evans.

Ramsden, Pamela. Top Team Planning. New York: John Wiley and Sons, 1973.

Rosen, John. Direct Analysis. New York: Grune & Stratton, 1953.

Russell, Joan. Creative Dance in the Primary School. New York: Fredrick Praeger, 1968.

Schilder, Paul. Brain and Personality. International Universities Press, 1951.

_____. The Image and Appearance of the Human Body. New York: John Wiley & Sons, Inc., 1964.

Schutz, William. Joy: Expanding Human Awareness. New York: Grove Press, 1968.

Sechehaye, Marguerite. Autobiography of a Schizophrenic Girl. New York: Grune and Stratton, 1965.

Sullivan, Harry Stack. Clinical Studies in Psychiatry. New York: W. W. Norton & Co.

Thass-Thienemann, Theodore. Symbolic Behavior. New York: Washington Square Press, Inc., 1968.

Turner, Victor. The Ritual Process Structure and Anti-Structure. Chicago: Aldine Publishing Co., 1969.

Urban, William. The Draw a Person. Los Angeles: Western Psychological Services, 1973.

Wallace, Anthony. Culture and Personality. New York: Random House, 1969.

Whiting, John. "Socialization Process and Personality." In Francis Hsu (Ed.), Psychological Anthropology. Dorsey Press, Inc., 1961, pp. 355-380.

_____ and Child, Irwin. Child Training and Personality. New Haven: Yale University Press, 1953.

_____, _____ and Lambert, William. Field Guide for a Study of Socialization. New York: John Wiley and Sons, Inc., 1966.

Willard, Helen and Spackman, Clare. Occupational Therapy. Philadelphia: J.D. Lippincott Company, 1963.

Wolff, Werner. The Expression of Personality. New York: Harper and Bros., 1945.

Wolman, Benjamin Ed. Dictionary of Behavioral Science. New York: Van Nostrand Reinhold Company, 1973.

Articles and Unpublished Manuscripts

Adler, Janet. "The Study of an Autistic Child," American Dance Therapy Association Conference Proceedings, October 1968.

Bartenieff, Irmgard. "Effort Observation and Effort Assessment in Rehabilitation," Dance Notation Bureau Reprint, New York, 1962.

_____; Davis, Martha; and Paulay, Forestine. "Four Adaptations of Effort Theory in Research and Teaching," Dance Notation Bureau Reprint, New York, 1968.

_____. "Research in Anthropology: A Study of Dance Styles in Primitive Cultures," CORD, May, 1967

Bender, Lauretta and Boas, Franziska. "Creative Dance in Therapy," American Journal of Orthopsychiatry, April 1941.

Benedict, Ruth. "Child Rearing in Eastern European Countries," Personalities and Cultures, Robert Hunt (Ed.). New York: Natural History Press, 1967.

Bernstein, Penny. "Range of Response as seen Through a Developmental Progression." What is Dance Therapy Really? Govine and Smallwood Ed. ADTA, 1973.

_____. "Tension Flow Rhythms As a Developmental Diagnostic Tool Within the Theory of the Recapitulation of Ontogeny" Dance Therapy—Depth and Dimension. Delores Plunk Ed, ADTA, 1975.

Bernstein, Penny and Bernstein, Lawrence. "A Conceptualization of Group Dance-Movement Therapy as a Ritual Process" American Dance Therapy Association Monograpy III, 1974.

Bernstein, Penny and Cafarelli, Enzo. "An Electromyographical Validation of the Effort System of Notation." American Dance Therapy Association Monograpy II., 1973.

Bernstein, Penny; Garson, Blaine; Miller, Linda; and Horbalie, Marylin. "Pilot Study in the Use of Tension Flow System of Movement Notation in an Ongoing Study of Infants as Risk for Schizophrenic Disorders." Dance Therapy—Depth and Dimension. Delores Plunk Ed, ADTA, 1975.

Chace, M. "A Psychological Study as Applied to Dance," Presented at the American Psychological Association Meetings, New York, September, 1957.

_____. "Dance as an Adjunctive Therapy with Hospitalized Mental Patients," Bulletin of the Menninger Clinic, XVIX, November 1953, pp. 219-25.

Chace, M. "Dance as Communication: Its Use in Growth or Treatment Situations," (Unpublished manuscript).

_____ . "Measurable and Intangible Aspects of Dance Sessions," Music Therapy, VII (1957), pp. 151-156.

_____ . "Movement Communication with Children," American Dance Therapy Association Conference Proceedings, October, 1968.

_____ . "Rhythmic Action for Communication," Unpublished manuscript.

_____ . "The Role of the Psychiatric Nurse in Dance Sessions," St. Mary's Newsletter, VIII (October 1960), p. 8.

_____ . "Stimulation of Creative Forms in Patient Productions." Presented at the Southeastern Chapter of the National Association for Music Therapy, Columbia, South Carolina, March 7, 1958.

_____ . "Technique for the Use of Dance as a Group Therapy," Music Therapy, III (1954), pp. 62-67.

_____ . "Use of Dance Action in Group Setting." Presented at the American Psychiatric Association Meeting, Los Angeles, California, May 1943.

Chaiklin, Harris. "Research and the Development of a Profession," American Dance Therapy Association Conference Proceedings, October 27, 1968.

Condon, W.S. "Kinesic Research and Dance Therapy," American Dance Therapy Association Conference Proceedings, October 1968.

Dratman, Mitchell L. "Reorganization of Psychic Structures in Autism: A Study Using Body Movement Therapy," American Dance Therapy Association Conference Proceedings, October 27-29, 1967.

Duffy, E. "The Measurement of Muscular Tension as a Technique for the Study of Emotional Tendencies," American Journal of Psychology, XLIV (1932), pp. 146-162.

Dyrud, Jack; Chace, Marian; and Erdman, Jean. "The Meaning of Movement as Human Expression and as an Artistic Communication," American Dance Therapy Association Conference Proceedings, October 25-27, 1968.

Grindlach, Ralph. "Movement Research," CORD, May 26, 1961, Introduction.

Hanna, Judith. "Dance Field Research: Some Whys and African Wherefores," CORD, May 1967.

Harrington, Charles. "Sexual Differentiation in Socialization and Some Male Genital Mutilations," American Anthropologist, LXX (October, 1968).

Howe, Louisa. "Notes on a Freudian Formulation of Psychomotor Therapy." Unpublished manuscript.

James, William T. "A Study of the Expression of Bodily Posture," The Journal of Genetic Psychology, VII (1932), pp. 405-37.

Kalish, Beth. "Body Movement Therapy for Autistic Children," American Dance Therapy Association Conference Proceedings, October 1968.

Kestenberg, Judith. "Childhood and Adult Pathology," Journal of Hillside Hospital, XVII (April-July 1968).

_____ . "Rhythm and Organization in Obsessive-Compulsive Development," The International Journal of Psycho-Analysis, XLVII (1966), pp. 151-159.

_____ , "The Role of Movement Patterns in Development: I. Rhythms of Movement," Psychoanalytic Quarterly, XXXIV (1965), pp. 1-36.

_____ . "The Role of Movement Patterns in Development," Psychoanalytic Quarterly, XXXIV (1965), pp. 517-562.

_____ . "The Role of Movement Patterns in Development: III. The Control of Shape," Psychoanalytic Quarterly, XXXVI (1967), pp. 359-409.

_____ . "Self Environment and Objects as Seen Through the Study of Movement Patterns." Unprinted manuscript, 1969.

_____ . "Suggestions for Diagnostic and Therapeutic Procedures in Movement Therapy," American Dance Therapy Association Conference Proceedings, October 27-29, 1967.

Krout, Maurice. "A Preliminary Note on Some Obscure Symbolic Muscular Responses of Diagnostic Value in the Study of Normal Subjects," American Journal of Psychiatry, II (1931-2), pp. 29-71.

La Barre, Weston. "The Cultural Basis of Emotions and Gestures," Journal of Personality, XVI (1947), pp. 48-68.

Lippman, Paul. "Is There Life Before Death? Schizophrenia, Normality and Other Human Disasters." American Dance Therapy Association Conference Proceedings, October 1968.

Lowen, Alesander. "Breathing, Movement and Feeling." Lecture reprint, 1965.

_____ . "The Rhythm of Life." Lecture reprint, 1966.

_____ . "Sex and Personality." Lecture reprint, 1962.

_____ . "Thinking and Feeling." Lecture reprint, 1967.

Mosey, Anne. "Treatment of Pathological Distortion of Body Image," The American Journal of Occupational Therapy, XXIII (September-October 1969).

Pesso, Albert. "Workshop on Psychomotor Therapy," American Dance Therapy Association Conference Proceedings, October 1968.

Salome-Finkelstein. "An Experimental Psychological Study of the Kinetic Pattern in Schizophrenia," Psychiatria Neurologia Neurochirurgia, LXVII (1964), pp. 182-186.

Schmals, Claire and White, Elissa. "Movement Analysis for Dance Therapists," American Dance Therapy Association Conference Proceedings, 1969.

Workshops and Courses

Bartenieff, Irmagard. Lectures from "Effort-Shape." Teachers College, Columbia University: 1969 summer session.

Chace, Marian. Dance Therapy Workshop. Turtle Bay School: June 1969.

Hill, Mildred. Workshop in Dance Therapy. Mariana Parra Studio: September 27, 1969.

Kestenberg, Judith. Lectures from the "Psychology of Movement." Dance Notation Bureau: September 1969-June 1970.

Schmals, Claire and White, Elissa. Workshop in Effort-Shape Dance Therapy. Dance Notation Bureau: September 8-12, 1969.

Films

Adler, Janet. Looking for Me. (Pennsylvania)

Bernstein, Penny. To Move is to be Alive: A Developmental Approach in Dance Movement Therapy. 16 mm. 30 min. B/W with sound. Produced by Pittsburgh Child Guidance Center, 1973.

Honig. Other Voices. (Pennsylvania).

Kalish, Beth. Film of Dance Therapy with an Autistic Child. (Pennsylvania).

Warrendale. (Canadian Documentary Film).

222

INDEX

V

Vernon, 2
Vestibular perception, 126-129
Vibratory perception, 124-126

W

Weaning Ritual, 110, 112-113
Work, 136-138